A Catalogue of Sins

A Catalogue of

SINS

A Contemporary Examination of
Christian Conscience

by William F. May

Holt, Rinehart and Winston

New York   Chicago   San Francisco

Published simultaneously in Canada by Holt, Rinehart
and Winston of Canada, Limited.

Library of Congress Catalog Card Number: 66-13494

First Edition

Chapter 4, "The Sin Against the Brother: Envy," and Chapter 7, "The Sin
Against the Friend: Betrayal," have appeared prior to publication respec-
tively in *Christianity and Crisis* and *Cross Currents.*

Grateful acknowledgment is extended to the following for their kind per-
mission to include excerpts from the publications listed:

The Bodley Head Ltd., London, for an excerpt from Dante's *Inferno,*
translated by John D. Sinclair.

The Journal of Religion, for an excerpt from "A Christian Approach to
the Question of Sexual Relations Outside of Marriage," by Paul Ramsey,
XLV, No. 2 (April 1965).

Prayer Book Press, Hartford, Connecticut, for an excerpt taken from the
High Holiday Prayer Book, edited by Rabbi Morris Silverman.

The Viking Press Inc., for a short excerpt from *A Portrait of the Artist as
a Young Man* by James Joyce, copyright 1916 by B. W. Huebsch, Inc., 1944
by Nora Joyce; copyright © 1964 by the Estate of James Joyce. All rights
reserved.

Unless otherwise noted, the Scripture quotations in this publication are
from the Revised Standard Version of the Bible, copyrighted 1946 and 1952.

Designer: Ernst Reichl
8573008
Printed in the United States of America

For Beverly

Foreword

Since the sin of ingratitude has been omitted from the list of vices considered in this book, it would be embarrassing to commit it in the Foreword by failing to acknowledge the very substantial help and encouragement I have had in preparing this volume.

I am particularly grateful to colleagues in the Religion Department and to the administration of Smith College for a sabbatical year, 1963–64, during the course of which this book was developed. Additional support came from the Committee on Aid to Faculty Research and Publication of Smith College and from the Lilly Foundation Post-doctoral Fellowship Program. Further, the faculties and library staffs of the Kirchliche Hochschule, West Berlin, Germany, and of St. Mary's College, St. Andrews University, St. Andrews, Scotland, permitted me to work in much-treasured privacy in their respective facilities during the course of my sabbatical leave.

I am indebted to Mr. Wayne Cowan, Managing Editor of *Christianity and Crisis,* for his encouragement of my work across the years. An essay on envy, originally written for that journal, prompted this volume and appears here now in an expanded form.

Mlle. Marthe Sturm, Professor Emeritus of Smith College, read portions of the manuscript with care; A. Lewis Soens, Assistant Professor at Notre Dame University, gave the whole a final critical reading; but, in addition to these persons, I must especially thank Professor Arthur C. McGill of the Religion Department, Princeton University, who read the manuscript in its later stages and offered many helpful suggestions concerning design and detail that have been incorporated in the finished book.

Working with Mr. Joseph Cunneen, Director of the Religion

Department, Holt, Rinehart and Winston, more briefly with his former associate, Mr. William Robert Miller, and most recently with Mrs. Joyce Reisinger of that firm, has taught me the advantages of having a thoroughly professional group of editors in the field.

William F. May

Indiana University
February 1967

Contents

A Catalogue of Sins

Introduction

This book is about the several sins rather than about the sinfulness of man. I will attempt to exhibit each sin in its experiential detail and variety as it actually assaults human beings in the flesh. In this respect, the book is a little closer to the efforts of the medieval moralists and the liberal Protestant preachers of the nineteenth century (despite their much publicized lack of a doctrine of the sinfulness of man) than to the doctrinal constructions of modern neo-orthodoxy. In the latter the emphasis fell on *sin* rather than on the *sins*; there was more reflection about the sinfulness of man than about the plurality of its forms. Admittedly there were exceptions: Kierkegaard described with clinical detail the varieties of despair, and Reinhold Niebuhr wrote brilliantly about the complexities of pride, sensuality, and dishonesty. All too often, however, reference to the sins disappeared into the abstraction, "Sin," without convincing us that it had reference to the heart's own affliction before God.

All such talk about sin apart from its various forms suffers from the danger of saying at once too little and too much; sin is simultaneously underestimated and overestimated. It is underestimated when it is abstracted from its concrete expressions. Its reality thins out. It dissipates and vanishes, not because it has been truly vanquished by a power that takes its measure, but because this very approach is too indeterminate to uncover it. Sin exists only in the concrete and never as an abstract whole. Like a guerrilla army, it can never be seen in its entirety. When an expedition is sent out against it, it vanishes into thin air, only to return when no one is looking. It resists the pedantry of those who seek to organize against it as a whole.

To consider sin apart from the sins also runs the opposite risk of overestimating its power, as though it were a positive lump of reality with a place in the world by the will and intention of God. Although sin may have a certain common essence that expresses itself in all particular sins, it is grossly inflated whenever it is reified or deified. Sin is not one of the provisions of God, like stars, trees, and mother's milk. Nor is it a darkling god in its own right, to which a kind of religious deference is due. It ought not to have a place in the cosmos beyond its desert. Unfortunately, there is a widespread form of piety (not at all confined to the Christian church) that derives all its religious satisfaction from sin. Hosts of gloomy critics are predisposed to see nothing but human failure around them. Their prayers and meditations begin and end with the brokenness of the human condition. Devotees of what Karl Rahner has called the sin-mysticism of our age, they are prone to find disease more fascinating than health, diagnosis more satisfying than cure, sin more alive than grace.

Of the two errors, however, the more fundamental is the first. When sin is overestimated, it is actually converted into something less than itself; in the long run, therefore, it is underestimated. Dramatized, exaggerated and deified, it is also volatilized and abstracted from its actual power to damage a man's life in God. Its true deadliness is overlooked. Sin exaggerated quickly passes over into sin underestimated, because something other than sin stimulates the imagination and moves the emotions to pity and terror.

Needless to say, there is no advance guarantee that a book devoted to the sins, rather than to sin, will avoid, in any given instance, the dangers of false appraisal. Victorians, for example, exaggerated the import of lust and sloth in their lives while underestimating the destructive power of envy and avarice. But if we deal concretely with a particular sin as it actually violates a man's life in God, we should be able to avoid—at least in principle—the sort of false appraisal that results from theological abstraction. This means that we will have to go out from the compound of systematic theology and into the bush country of the heart to the actual site of sin's disclosure.

In method, this book is a venture in problematic rather than systematic theology. I have tried to explore each sin in its own terms—taking up the question of its structure, its scope, its guises, its deadliness, its fecundity, and its appeal—rather than to subordinate each of the sins to the demands of a systematic whole. The result is a series of relatively autonomous essays.

Traditional systematic theology, by its very nature, discouraged the production of discrete, independent essays. Chapters in a book were inevitably written from the vantage point of a single perspective, called the "Christian point of view." This point of view could be organized, interpreted, contrasted, and defended, in whole or in part, in relation to other points of view.

The methods of systematic theology are not fully appropriate to a book on the several sins—and this for two important reasons. First, the man who says he has a "point of view" on such a subject usually lays down an unreal spiritual distance between the human realities he is describing and the vantage point from which he describes them. He is more tempted to argue the superiority of his position than to confess his sins. It is difficult to overcome the pedantry of his distance—even when propositions concerning sin are meticulously universalized to include the viewer himself. Reinhold Niebuhr recognized this problem in *The Nature and Destiny of Man.* He sensed the ironic danger of falling into spiritual pride over precisely that article of faith that ought to discourage it—the doctrine of sin. Therefore, he restricted Christians to a rather peculiar relationship to their much-treasured biblical point of view by appeal to the notion of "having and not having" the truth. This phrase was a way of suggesting that Christians do not *have* a point of view in such a way as to be exempt from its judgments. Instead of resorting to Niebuhrian paradox, however, it might be better to abandon altogether the notion of a "point of view," with its assumption of a certain distance between the viewer and the veiwed, as a description of the way in which the Christian is related to the truth.

Systematic theology suffers from a second liability in its approach to the subject of sin. It tends to organize the items under its purview into patterns abstracted from their moving force. Systematic theology has a bias in favor of the still life, the ordered landscape. God is still; man is still; even the devil holds his breath. Father, Son, and Holy Spirit occupy their assigned places in the triptychally organized whole. This careful picture, however, is simply not the world the Christian knows in the flesh. He knows sin in the surprise of grace; he knows God while wrestling with demons. He has no magic wand with which to wave each power back into its place. To approach sin (or grace, for that matter) against the backdrop of a total Christian landscape with each item in its place may be precisely the way to miss sin as it catches a man off-balance and without his maps.

Theology more suitable to the subject of this book has to be problematic rather than systematic. The word "problem" by origin refers to a task, a challenge, or a puzzle, not always intellectual in character. The importance of the elements of movement, interaction, and struggle in its meaning comes through in many of the associations of the Greek term *problema*. Literally it meant a gage thrown down (in the course of a challenge to a fight or contest). Or again, it meant a jutting promontory or barrier and, conversely, a shield or barrier erected against a particular attack. Quite understandably, Huizinga, in *Homo Ludens*, argued for a connection between *problema* in its intellectual meaning as a riddle or puzzle and its meaning in the world of contest and even war.

Correspondingly, a theological problem cannot be treated as a static item or object held together with others in a total field of vision. Independently intriguing, it draws one to itself, inviting exploration of its own structural elements and idiosyncrasies. Like a riddle, it may not be solved simply on the basis of rules learned elsewhere. This does not mean that all knowledge previously acquired is irrelevant, but that it must be wholly subordinate and sensitive to the task or challenge at hand.

I have no intention of resting theology on etymology, least of all on the origins and meanings of one word. But perhaps some of the associations of the word "problem" help to interpret the way in which this book has been written. The attempt was made to treat each sin within the terms of its own unfolding rather than to maintain a single optical vantage point on them all. A "problem" does not always permit the use of insights gained elsewhere. For this reason, I have attempted to make each essay relatively autonomous in order to react to the peculiarities of each of the sins—for each presents its own special challenge, not only to the understanding but to the soul.

Sin
and the Sins

Sin is *whatever we do that violates our life in God.* An expanded diagram of this definition should help us see the inadequacy of sentimental, moralistic, legalistic, and abstractly theological approaches to the subject.

1) Sin is whatever we do that *violates* . . . This aspect of the definition is designed to protect against a sentimental reduction of sin to human foible. Sin is a real violation of humanity in its wholeness and integrity, not just a name for a set of endearing human weaknesses that fill out one's character. "My Sin" is not the name of a perfume that supplements my personality in its allure. It stands for whatever I do that mars, mauls, inflates, depresses, disrupts, distorts, or abandons humanity. The word "violate" is related to violence, and refers to massive damage and destruction. Sin is ultimately destructive of the human.

There are two ways in which sin can be sentimentally interpreted as a fulfillment of one's humanity: first, and most obviously, when it is reduced to a casual foible that serves to enrich the total impression of one's character; second, when it is elevated into a tragic necessity through which one's deepest human aspirations are fulfilled. The latter is German idealism of the nineteenth century against a background of Wagnerian trombones. In both kinds of sentimentality, the assumption is the same: innocent humanity is bland and colorless. It must go through phases of conflict and estrangement to reach its fulfillment. Violence, therefore, is not sinful violation. It is part of

that total dynamic process by which (albeit poignantly and tragically) humanity reaches its full coloration and perfection.

There is, of course, a certain truth to the sentimentalist's approach to sin. Although sin is destructive, some sins nevertheless
have a fragrance that masks their ultimate effects. This fragrance is apt to disturb the judgment and make the act itself
seem either trivial or tragically necessary. Meanwhile, the sin
becomes so intertwined with one's whole person as to seem
not worth fighting. Whether foible or fate, it no longer appears
alien and destructive to one's being.

Unfortunately, the Christian community has often encouraged
a reverse sort of setimentality in which foible and fate are
falsely elevated into sin. Many acts which the overpious Christian
interprets as sinful are, rather, temperamental faults, tragic necessities, or public events wholly beyond his control; they should be
laughed at—or cried over—not confesed. When the Christian
falsely confesses them, he exploits confession to prove his moral
sensitivity and his good intentions. His confession discredits its
own seriousness by appropriating everything to itself. Underneath, he does not really think of himself as a sinner; in fact, he
considers himself a rather good fellow for knowing his own (for-
givable) weaknesses and failures or for his willingness to accept
personal responsibility for the shortcomings of the entire community.

At the core of any such pietistic version of sin is a good deal of
self-idealization. Sin is sentimentalized if it is reduced to what I
would like to forgive and would find no obstacle to forgiving.
God's forgiveness then comes as no surprise; indeed, his refusal to
forgive would be a moral shock. It is heartless of God to refuse to
forgive what I would forgive, were I in his place. Thus, beneath
the toadying humility of the confession lurks a barely concealed
pretension to divinity. The self lavishly overestimates itself—not
with respect to its power, but surely with respect to its virtues. It
dissolves sin in a quivering moral sensitivity.

2) Sin is whatever we do that violates our life *in God*. This
second element in the definition distinguishes sin from moral
evil. The two are related. Each of the seven deadly sins, for

example, involves its share of moral evil. The man of pride,
envy, malice, or lust damages both himself and his neighbor. But
this damage is not what makes the act sinful. Sin has to do with
God. In each of the sins, a man acts in such a way as to make his
relationship to God precarious, frightened, suspicion-laden, and
deceitful. A catalogue of sins is not quite the same thing as a
catalogue of vices. To be sure, the ways in which a man estranges
himself from God include those ways in which he does violence
to his neighbor. As the Christian tradition has insisted, his vices
are also his sins. But his vices are not vices alone precisely because he has done his violence as a creature of God, before God,
and against God.

The afternoon prayers for the Jewish service on the Day of
Atonement express and repeat with each phrase the decisive element in sin. The prayers take up a whole range of human vice,
but, in each case, the accent falls on the fact that the deed was
performed "before Thee":

> For the sin which we have committed before Thee
>   by casting off the yoke of Thy commandments,
> And for the sin which we have committed before Thee
>   by contentiousness;
> For the sin which we have committed before Thee
>   by ensnaring our neighbor,
> And for the sin which we have committed before Thee
>   by envy;
> For the sin which we have committed before Thee
>   by levity,
> For the sin which we have committed before Thee
>   by being stiff-necked;
> For the sin which we have committed before Thee
>   by running to do evil,
> And for the sin which we have committed before Thee
>   by talebearing;
> For the sin which we have committed before Thee
>   by vain oaths,
> And for the sin which we have committed before Thee
>   by causeless hatred;

For the sin which we have committed before Thee
    by the breach of trust,
And for the sin which we have committed before Thee
    with confusion of mind;
For all these, O God of forgiveness, forgive us,
    pardon us, grant us atonement. *

Sin is what a man is compelled to confess to God because his
action, whatever its immediate content may be, has placed him
in crisis before God. Our use of the term "sin," therefore, indicates that this book is not a general work on human vice, and
certainly not a Christian commentary on the moral and religious
failings of non-Christians. A study of sin can never venture too
far from one's own confession and the confession of one's own
people. During prayer, and particularly during the prayer of the
confession of sins, it is spiritually shabby to stare at others.

3) Sin is *whatever* we do that violates our *life in God*. This
element in the definition provides against a legalistic approach to
the subject. Legalists define sin as disobeying the commands of
God or, even more abstractly, violating Christian principles.
Most traditional catalogues of sins, both Roman Catholic and
Protestant, were legalistic. To identify a sin meant to show how
it entailed the breach of a divine law, derived from either a
command of God, a rule of the church, or the order of nature.

There are several reasons why legalism is inadequate on the
subject of sin. First, and most important, the legalist usually
assumes that the law is man's only serious point of contact with
God. Only through the law does God communicate himself to
creatures. He is like a much-absent father, distant and remote
from his children, who comes alive for them only at one point—
when he clears his throat, deepens his voice, and commands them
to obey. Such legalism offers an impoverished understanding of
man's participation in the life of God. It implicitly denies that
man has been created to enjoy the presence of God in a way that
a son might enjoy the presence of a good and undistracted father,
a wife the life of her husband, or a citizen the common good of

* Morris Silverman (ed.), *High Holiday Prayer Book* (Hartford, Conn.:
Prayer Book Press Publishers, 1951), p. 199.

his country. The legalist has contact only with a solemnity that imposes on him a set of commands and a few hints at punishment; his God is reduced to a specter who hovers elusively on the other side of the law that fences him in. It is difficult to take seriously a violation of one's life in God if participation in his life has been reduced to mere legality.

The Prophets of the Old Testament sought to avoid this reduction of sin to legal abstraction. That is why sin was described so often as an act of adultery.* For the Prophets, God is not a remote employer who hedges in his employee with rules, while he busies himself with other projects. He is husband to Israel. He found her in the field when she was nothing to look at, and washed her, and told her to live; and he took her to be his own. He promised himself to her and made love to her, and adorned her as his bride, lavishing upon her the riches of his love and his life. Israel grew and prospered under the hand of God, but she went whoring after other gods. Her sin, therefore, is adultery, which is not simply the breaking of a rule (although it is that) but the violation of the very substance of one's life in the life of another. Sin is not simply disobedience—it is infidelity.

At the same time that we reject the lawyer's approach to sin, we must avoid the error of those Protestant romanticists who systematically deny to God a living presence in and through command. Rules in themselves are not evil. The good news of the Gospel does not invariably mean a life without form and structure, a freedom beyond law and principle. If legalists impoverish the life of God by reducing him to the law alone, antinomians make him into a formless vitality. No father is close to children if they know him only in the solemnity of his command, but he may be equally elusive for them if they never encounter his imperative presence. God should not be softened into the formless receptivity of the modern nondirective counsellor: there are occasions when his voice is concentrated in a simple *do* or *don't*.

Legalism should be rejected for a second reason related to the first; it almost invariably overlooks the worst of sins, the

* Ezekiel 16.

sins of the self-righteous. It is obsessed with the sins of the law-breakers but blind to the sins of the law-keepers. It condemns the adulterers, the murderers, the thieves, and the tax collectors, but ignores the pride of those respectable people who control the machinery of condemnation. Legalism encourages men to boast of their spiritual sufficiency before God, and thus further alienates them from the source of their life in God. Their rebellion against God is more radical and total than that of the lawless.

D. R. Davies provided a helpful analogy when he observed that sin is more like the act of a traitor than the act of a criminal.* The rebellion of a criminal against the laws of his country is quite limited. No matter how spectacular his crimes, he breaks only certain specific laws. A traitor, by comparison, commits the far more serious offense of contesting altogether the sovereignty of his country. Analogously, the sinner is distinguished, not so much by the particular laws that he has broken but by the fact that he denies altogether the right of God to rule.

Both analogies used in this section on legalism—sexual betrayal and political treason—converge in the word that Calvin chose for his primary definition of sin: infidelity. Sin is like treason; sin is like adultery; in summary, sin is infidelity. Adultery can be said to characterize sin only because it is already acknowledged that God is husband to Israel or that Christ is bridegroom to the church. Likewise, treason can be said to characterize sin only because it is already acknowledged that God is the king of Israel or that Christ fulfills the royal office in the Kingdom of God. Each of these analogies for God's relationship to his people presupposes the imparting of life and blessing from one side to another and the subsequent violation of its reception. The wife receives her well-being from her husband, the citizen his substance from the wealth and might and favor of his king. In both cases, sin is infidelity.

The metaphorical character of the biblical language ought not

* D. R. Davies, *Down Peacock's Feathers* (New York: Macmillan, 1946), p. 49; as cited by Bernhard Anderson, *Rediscovering the Bible* (New York: Association Press, 1951), p. 75.

to frighten us away from its use. Since a theist cannot describe God's relationship to the world without resorting to analogies, how can he avoid them in a description of that relationship when it is spoiled? Even if one preferred a more neutral term for the description of sin than infidelity, what would it be? The rejection of God? Rejection, in its root, refers to something thrown that has been thrown back. The term may be helpful for the understanding of sin, but not because it is free of metaphor. The same thing can be said for the denial of God, rebellion, disobedience, unbelief, corruption, and other traditional words and phrases used to define sin.

Although infidelity is not the only valid analogy for the characterization of sin, it has a special value in describing the context in which the other attitudes of sin occur. Man's neglect of God is not like the incidental inattentiveness of a child to his piano lessons, but rather that of a man to the very source of his being and well-being; and deadness toward God is not the lethargy of a man or a machine run down, but rather the deadness of a marriage played out.

The analogy of infidelity is also extremely useful in gathering up important elements in the definition of sin. As opposed to a sentimental approach in which sin is trivialized, the analogies of adultery and treason leave no doubt that real damage has been done, a violence absorbed. Unlike a moralistic approach, the analogies make it clear that this violence—whatever else it may entail—represents a rupture of man's relationship with God. And as opposed to a legalistic understanding of sin, the analogies specify this rupture as a violation of the very terms of one's life subsisting in the life of God.

4) Sin is whatever we do that violates *our life* in God. This element in the definition guards against an abstractly theological notion of sin, as though it were a crisis of man before God, abstracted from a third factor: the human environment upon which sin exercises itself. A man does not meet God, much less evade God, in an encounter isolated from his world and the neighbor. The Penitential Psalms of the Old Testament and the prayers for the Day of Atonement reach down into the grit of human life

when they talk about sin. Even the Apostle Paul, who subjected the doctrine to its most rigorous and abstractly theological statement, found it important to include tables of vices in some of his letters. The term sin does not refer to a special class of offenses against God (ritual, theological) as opposed to offenses against the neighbor and the world (moral, aesthetic, and technical). To think of sin as God-oriented alone tends to confer upon the sinner a satanic height that is not his. It suggests that his rejection of God is pure rejection, without a rasping effect on himself, other selves, and the world.

The attempt to abstract sin from its full human matrix has consequences also for the study of sin. If sin is an offense against God alone, wholly abstracted from neighbor and environment, then it would appear that the theologian alone is competent to deal with the subject. Sin is his private reserve and preserve. If this is the case, then the novelist, the psychoanalyst, the etymologist, the physician, and the lawyer have no light to throw upon the subject. Fallen angels, not men, are the offenders. But if sin, in fact, involves additionally and inseparably the harsh, abrasive, twisting, and devious action of a man against his environment, then insights may be accepted from other sources. What Freud had to say about the oral and the anal stages of development may help to extend the medieval tradition on the sins of gluttony and avarice. What the etymologists have to say about the roots of words in the common tradition may help to cut through the overlay of centuries of Christian moralizing that is no longer in contact with the sins in their experiential power and allure. There is no need to fear that the Christian message will be automatically compromised by its use of insights from other sources on a subject that so intertwines itself with every aspect of the human.

The basis for the pluralization of the sins

It is possible to pluralize the sins in two basic ways: either by beginning with the complexity of God and his relationship to his creatures or with the complexity of man and his diverse involvements with the world and his fellows.

If one begins with God, several options present themselves. First and most obviously, one might begin with the plurality of divine commands and distinguish the several sins according to the laws disobeyed in each case. This is the procedure that Thomas Aquinas and (even more strictly) some of the Reformers followed in the delineation of the several sins. Quite naturally, they used the Ten Commandments as an organizing table to keep the sins from proliferating indefinitely. When abstracted from all else, such an approach can produce a somewhat pedantic and spectral legalism, but, as we have seen, there is no need to avoid imperative statement altogether, as though the law were inherently and irremediably profane.

Second, one might begin, not with a series of commands from God to his creatures, but with the very being of God in whom these commands are rooted. The being of God expresses itself in a variety of perfections that define his life. This is what Scripture meant by the glory of God. Sin immediately pluralizes itself in the various ways in which men fall short of the divine glory; that is, by counterfeiting and contradicting God in one of his various perfections. This was the method of Augustine, who recognized in each of the sins a prideful attempt to mimic one of the attributes of God. Thus wastefulness parodies the divine generosity; avarice, God's possession of all things; anger, the judgment of God, and so forth. Augustine's approach has the advantage of rooting commands in the life of God himself. The imperative in each case is the imperative of his presence, and sin is the specific contradiction of that presence in one aspect of its perfection.

But Augustine, in his early writings at least, lacked focus on the concrete acts of God in which he makes himself known in his perfections. Thus his *Confessions,* despite their celebration of the providence of God, are shot through with a mystic yearning for an immediacy with God not yet experienced. The sinner, in effect, is judged by a presence which he does not yet fully know and enjoy. God's presence becomes the goal rather than the point of departure of the Christian life. The several sins are, therefore, not really man's contradiction of God's effective presence, but a series of lapses by which a man fails to arrive at this presence. Given this view of the Christian life, it was quite natural to develop a hierarchy of sins. The Christian life itself was a matter of vertical ascent toward a goal, and sins could be gauged on the basis of their power to impede a man's progress toward his destination in God.

Third, one might begin with the concrete acts of God, in which he discloses the fullness of his life and perfections. This approach assumes that God has made himself known in a series of acts refulgent with his life and power. The Gospel is nothing but witness and testimony to this series of events, and the several sins are nothing but the plurality of ways in which men contradict this presence so disclosed. This approach is a little closer to that of the later Augustine and of those identified with the modern resurgence of biblical theology. The example of Karl Barth will suffice.

The twentieth-century Swiss theologian forgoes the attempt to define God on the basis either of divine law or of religious experience. He defines God entirely on the basis of a threefold action toward his creatures in Christ. God's saving work is threefold; correspondingly, the forms of sin are threefold. God's downward movement of humiliation in the Son is sinfully contradicted in the upward thrust of human pride. Jesus' upward movement of exaltation and victory receives its sinful contradiction in the downward thrust of man in sloth. Finally, God's truthful disclosure of himself in Christ is contradicted in the sin of falsehood. Thus pride, sloth, and falsehood, these three, are the forms of sin, Christologically defined. Barth's approach has the advantage of recognizing that sin is not so much a contradiction of the command to be good as a contradiction of the Good itself, not so much a lapse from its future enjoyment as an obstinacy before its present disclosure.

Once the several sins are seen in this light, of course, one can understand why Protestants have usually refused to rank the sins according to the order of their deadliness and seriousness. Insofar as each of the sins is truly a sin, it breaks defiantly, obstinately, and mindlessly—and equally—against the hard rock of God's presence *already* effective in the Savior. There is no ground for calculating the degree to which a given act threatens to deprive one of a future enjoyment. At the same time, this understanding of sin so emphasizes the effective presence of God in Jesus Christ that it tends to make the sinful act seem something that no sensible person could perform—more so than it is. Barth's approach overlooks the sinner's experience of the temptingness of sin, a temptingness grounded in his sense of the absence of God and in the credibility of the description of the world which sin presents.

Therefore this book will begin with man rather than with God, in its attempt to approach the sins in their diversity. This is not to reject on principle the attempts to begin with the command of God, the being of God, or the act of God in Jesus Christ, but simply to restrict the special theme of this book to sin in all its human allure.

There are at least two ways of beginning with man. The traditional approach is best represented by Thomas Aquinas. He located the various sins within the framework of a faculty psychology. Considered naturally, man is a composite of three faculties—reason, will, and appetite—hierarchically related to one another, with reason in command. Each of the sins can be traced back to a certain excess or defect of passion, by which the right rule of reason is disordered. Thus lust and gluttony have their distinctive grounds in an excessive desire for pleasure; envy and sloth in an excess of sorrow; fearlessness and daring in a defect of the emotion of fear, and so forth.

Within this framework it was possible for Thomas to account for the diversity and attractiveness of sin. Man is a complex rather than a simple being. He can direct himself to any one of a variety of goods—food, clothing, shelter, sexual intercourse, defense, or education, for example—all of them related to a legitimate aspect of his being and yet each, if pursued alone as the Supreme Good, with impoverishing effect on the whole man. The key moral question for Thomism is the teleological question: What is the *chief end* of man? What is that Supreme Good in which the whole man will find his fulfillment and, therefore, to which all other goods may be legitimately subordinate, each in its place? The answer, of course, is God, in whom human nature is fulfilled. Sin, accordingly, is a failure to direct oneself toward the chief goal of human existence by seeking one's Supreme Good in a lesser good. Herein lies the explanation both for sin's diversity and its appeal. The diversity of sin is simply the abundance of objects that men may substitute for that single object in which their nature can be fully satisfied. Not that all other objects are evil. Indeed, precisely because they are goods, man may be disposed to organize his life about one of them as his pre-eminent good and so give himself to one of the vices. Herein lies the logic of sin's appeal.

The approach to man adopted in this book differs from that of the Thomists. No attempt will be made either to trace the sins back to a faculty psychology or to orient them toward a ruling concept of the destiny of man. We will begin, not with the question of the *ends* of human life, but rather with its *givens.* And in exploring these givens, we will be less concerned with the *faculties* a man possesses than with the *situations* in which he finds himself. Man is inextricably in the world and with his neighbors, and many of the sins pluralize themselves in these involvements. We will not trace the sins back to an imbalance in the passions but track them out into that environment which they twist and reshape.

The sins of man with his world

The sins of man with his world are those of false worship, false fear, and false mastery. More traditionally, they have been called the sins of impurity of heart (idolatry), faintheartedness, and avarice. The first two sins are those of man in his vulnerability before the powers of the world in which he finds himself. They might be called the special sins of the man who is "religious" in his relationship to the world. Instead of living in the world, he falls under the thrall of the world. Either he falls under the spell of powers that he finds positive and fulfilling (Exodus 32), or he recoils in fright before powers that he finds overwhelming (Deuteronomy 1). In the sin of idolatry, the Israelites dance enthralled around the golden calf; in the sin of faintheartedness, they sicken with apprehension before the terrors of entrance into the promised land. The third sin is the opposite of the first two, the special vice of the man who seeks to reduce the world exclusively to his ownership and control. The biblical tradition comes closest to describing it in discussions of the capital sin of avarice. This is the sin of false activity and mastery, the special temptation of the secular man.

All three sins have been prefixed with the word "false" because passivity and activity, vulnerability and mastery, are not modes of relationship to the world that are in and of themselves sinful. There is good reason for the attitudes of awe before the heavens and fear before death; and there is an equally valid warrant for the attempt to master one's daily needs. To ignore the truth of these attitudes is to confuse the very conditions of creaturely existence with sin. Futhermore, it is to overlook the power of the sins themselves, since they are rarely maintained by falsehood alone. Each sin is fathered by falsehood, but its mother always is a certain truth.

The sins of man with his neighbor

There are more offenses against the neighbor than the brace of sins included in this section: envy, hatred, neglect, betrayal, and lust. Enough should have been covered, however, to suggest the way in which still others might be approached. Each sin is analyzed, not by tracing it back to that emotion whose excess or defect it represents (hatred, envy, lust, suspicion, and so forth) but by tracing it out into that particular social relation (to the brother, friend, enemy, needy, etc.) which is its typical setting. Envy is pre-eminently the sin against the brother; hatred, the sin against the enemy; neglect, the sin against the needy; betrayal, the sin against the friend; and lust, the sin against the sexual partner. These correlations are not rigid. It is possible to be malicious toward friends, or envious of enemies. But this does not destroy the importance of typical social relations in which they root and upon which they flourish.

This approach through social setting is somewhat older than its recent association with existentialism and a so-called "relational anthropology." The legal literature of the Bible itself classifies both duties and offenses according to certain archetypal social relations. The stranger, the wife, the servant, the friend, the brother, and the orphan focus and symbolize certain important human problems, even when a society is no longer nomadic or agarian in its structure. The figure of the father, for example, to cite an instance omitted from this series of essays, focuses all those problems that cluster around a man's relationship to authority. Luther recognized this focus when he discussed the widest range of problems connected with civil authority while interpreting the Fourth Commandment. We do not need to swallow Luther's paternalism on domestic and civic affairs to recognize the validity of the symbol. The sin of ingratitude, after all, is a state of numbness, uneasiness, and resentment directed toward all those to whom we are beholden. Their aid, however well-intended, humiliates us with a sense of our weakness and mortality. The sin of ingratitude extends backward and upward toward all those in positions of responsibility, but it focuses most keenly in the father. In like fashion, still other sins omitted from this series might be traced back to that social relation decisive for the man in its throes.

The social sins can be distinguished not only by the human situation in which each most typically emerges but also by the special ways in which they disrupt man's relationship to his neighbor. This disruption can be prepositionally defined. Man has been placed *in* his world, but *with* his neighbor. The preposition *with* expresses very simply what theologians have seen in the Genesis account of creation.* It was not good for man to be

---

* See Karl Barth, *Church Dogmatics*, ed. G. W. Bromiley and T. F. Torrance (12 Vols.; Edinburgh: T. & T. Clark, 1956), Vol. III, Pt. II, par. 45.

alone. He was created with his helpmate. He is intended for a relationship to his partner which is one of help, comfort, companionship, and joy. This placement is regulative not only for the relation to the sexual partner, but also for other relations in their less intimate ways.

Measured against this placement *with*, the disruption of sin can be prepositionally stated. In envy, instead of living *with* the neighbor, a man wants to be *in the place of* the neighbor. In hatred, instead of living *with* the neighbor, a man moves *against* the neighbor. In neglect, instead of living *with* the neighbor, a man seeks to live *without* the neighbor. In betrayal, instead of dealing *with* the neighbor, a man operates *behind the back* of the neighbor. In lust, instead of being intimate *with* the neighbor, a man is intimate *in spite of* the neighbor.

It is, of course, possible to interpret the social dimensions of other sins prepositionally. In avarice and pride a man seeks to place himself *over* the neighbor or to *withdraw from* him; in the deadness of sloth, he seeks to *let down* the neighbor; and, in deceit, he seeks to *hide from* the neighbor his own true location. In the various disruptions cited here, the most serious, in a sense, is the attempt to be *without* the neighbor. For the ultimate destination of every act *against, over, in the place of,* and *behind the back of* the neighbor is the intention to do *without* him.

Clearly there are limitations in this method of social analysis. It does not permit classification of the sins along lines coterminous with the great public-policy issues of our time (education, housing, segregation, population explosion, genetic controls, nuclear weapons and so forth). Correspondingly, no attempt has been made to be prescriptive in these areas. This series of essays deals with the personal modes of appropriation of social experience rather than with questions of social policy; with the content of confession rather than with the strategies of legislation.

In this respect, the book is intended to supplement, without supplanting, the social gospel and the neo-orthodox movements in Protestantism. Moralists in these movements focused on issues of social policy. In a time of overriding public crisis it was natural for them to do this. They were atoning for the sins of omission of traditional Protestant piety insofar as it harped on questions of personal vice and virtue at the expense of public justice. No moralist need be reminded today that a Victorian preoccupation with the personal virtues of industry, honesty, and integrity, at the expense of economic justice, made its own tragic contribution to the evils of our time.

Nevertheless, the moralist concerned with questions of policy cannot ignore those fundamental ways in which men appropriate social experience. Hatred, envy, betrayal, and neglect are not simply personal vices. Each implies a social syndrome, in conformity with which the contacts between persons and communities are patterned and interpreted. Neither the policy expert nor the pastor can afford to ignore these patterns.

Before anticipating the remaining sins, a concluding comment on the first two sets of vices and the anthropology which their analysis presupposes is required. I would not want to argue, along with some of the existentialists, that the concept of man can be altogether dissolved into the sum total of his involvements. It is impossible to define a man relationally without regard to those faculties or powers he must possess as a condition of relationship. At the very least, the terms of a man's involvement with the world and with his neighbor are that he is a creature of spirit and flesh.

Except as I am flesh and except as I can use my flesh instrumentally (feet for walking, hands for working), I could not relate to the world by way of mastery. I could not own and control fragments of the world except as I also own and control my own body. Again, except as I am flesh and except as my flesh is sensitive, susceptible, and vulnerable, I could not be open to the world as it pours in upon me in stars, dust, heat, thunder, exhaustion, cancer, and rain. I could not fall under the spell of a world that both enchants and terrifies me. My flesh therefore is more than instrumental, it is also the site for the disclosure of a world which I shall never be able to reduce to my property. Finally, except as I am flesh and except as my flesh is disclosive, I could not reveal myself to my neighbor. My flesh therefore is more than instrumental and more than vulnerable;

it is also revelatory; otherwise I could not be with my neighbor. At the same time, also, I am a creature of spirit. Except as I am spirit, I could not make use of my flesh as instrument or celebrate the discoveries of the flesh in its vulnerability, or stand revealed in the flesh to the neighbor. Except as I am spirit and flesh, the world and the neighbor could not be the very terms of my life that they are.

Thomas Aquinas is quite right, therefore, in recognizing that the sins have import for a man's right relation to his own flesh and spirit. We shall have occasion to recognize this dimension of sin as we proceed. But sin, in each case, is more than the accountable self (spirit and flesh) violating its own proper destiny before God; it is also a snarled relationship to the world and our neighbor. This book will trace these tangles.

The strategy and atmosphere of sin

The sins of deceit, craving, and anxiety are reminders that sins (especially deceit) can be the means to other sins or the cause of sins (especially craving and anxiety). While analyzed with these particular issues in mind, these sins cannot be interpreted in such a way as to leave the world and neighbors behind. Some have sought to distinguish sins against the neighbor from sins against one's self and have included lying among the latter. But it is difficult to abstract lying from the total involvement of the self with the world and the neighbor. This is true even of self-deceit. The distinguishing feature of deceit among the sins is not its orientation to the self alone, but rather its peculiar relation of service to the other sins. Unlike other of the traditional vices, lying is not an end in itself; it serves other ends. As such, it is peculiarly the utility sin. It is sin's strategy. Nevertheless, while deceit serves sin, it also uncovers the spiritual strain involved in sinning. Lying is at once the utility sin and the sign of sin's futility.

Sin can also be interpreted with reference to the troubled atmosphere in which all sins occur. Historically (and justifiably), the tradition has interpreted this atmosphere as craving and anxiety. The Middle Ages in particular saw man as a creature of boundless craving. The modern age tends to interpret him as a creature of unstanchable anxiety. Both ravenous desire and anxiety function as the breeding ground of sin and are special reminders that each of the sins breeds others.

The destination of sin

There are two sins that might be called the destination of sin, for they point to the goal of unimpeded sin in solitude and death. Pride is not solitude itself but the shadow of solitude; sloth is not death itself but the shadow of death come into possession of the soul.

Pride has been traditionally, and rightly, defined as the attempt to elevate the self above all others into the position of God. This rebellion against the Lord reaches its completion when not only God falls away, but all other lordly powers in creation bow down, like sheaves, before the solitary self. Earlier it was said that the final aim and intention of all the sins against the neighbor was to do *without* the neighbor. Pride is this final aim and intention of doing without. It is the sin of the first person singular, the "I," the solitary self.

If pride is man's rebellion against God in his lordship, sloth is deadness before God in his glory. Sloth is not the sleep of the lazy, it is the death of the bored. So understood, sloth is the destination of all man's sin, when the soul, once alive with desire, goes dead.

The glory of God means the life and splendor of God. Boredom brings to its completion man's original flight from the glory of God, to the glory of the world (idolatry), and then from the glory of the world to a final state of atrophy. Sloth is the soul at the end of the line, in a final state of spiritual death.

Starkly enough, the Christian looks for redemption in one who already occupies the destination of sin, in one who died, and died alone, on a cross.

The Sins of
Man with His World

1 False Worship:
IMPURITY OF HEART

When Gulliver was washed ashore in the land of the Lilliputians, the king sent two investigators to examine his person
and report items of a threatening nature that might be used by
the giant against his captors. In going through Gulliver's pockets
the investigators came across three articles of particular interest.
They described one as a great carpet, large enough to cover the
floor in the royal hall. What they had discovered, of course, was
Gulliver's handkerchief. The second, they said, was a mighty
engine with poles distended from it the size of the palisades
before the king's court. What they had found, in this case, was
Gulliver's comb. But the third item was the most baffling of all.
In a further recess of Gulliver's clothing they reported another
great engine that made a noise like a waterfall and had an invisible partition which prevented them from examining the monstrous figures on its face. It was, of course, Gulliver's watch. But
in writing their report to the king, the investigators said that it
was either a strange animal Gulliver had brought with him from
his own country, or his god—because he consulted it so often.
Swift, of course, is satirizing one of the gods of modern men—
mechanical time—but he is also describing what the real god of a

man is: whatever in his life he consults most often. John Calvin
once observed that man is distinguished from all other creatures
by the fact that he does not live without a religion. Man is an
incorrigible god-maker, a creature given to worship and adoration. Another way of putting the same thing is to say that he is a
manufacturer of idols. Man does not rid himself of religion when
he sins; quite the contrary, he reeks of it. He denies God by
falling under the spell of the world or one of its powers.

The argument of the first two chapters of this book is that it
is still meaningful to speak of contemporary man as a religious
being in his relationship to the world, and that we may therefore
discuss the special sins of the religious man. This argument cuts
across the current vogue of interpreting our age as "religionless,"
or "secular." If modern man is secular without qualification,
then an essay on idolatry (and the following essay on faintheartedness) is entirely out of place in a modern discussion of the
several sins. We could speak relevantly today only of the special
temptations and vices that beset the secular man.

What does it mean, however, to say that man, as a religious
being, denies God? To answer this question it will be necessary
to push out of the way familiar associations of the term with
official denominations and their developed theologies, and to
recover something of its original force. According to those who
can help us with the meaning of the word, religion consists,
first and foremost, of some sort of encounter with sacred power.

This power may appear in many different ways. For Israel,
sacred power meant the God who made a startling show of his
strength on behalf of the Israelites in a contest with the power of
the Pharaoh; who delivered his people from the hands of the
Egyptians by cunning and force; who published his will in commandments with compelling consequences for their future life;
and whose presence or absence, blessing or curse, was of critical
significance for every subsequent generation. For others, however,
the sacred may appear as something else. It may appear as Sex,
the Fertility of the soil, Revolution, or the State, whenever these
realities tower above all others as the capital in a man's life. Or

again, the sacred may disclose itself as Fate; it may appear as a reality that transcends and confounds all lesser realities from which men seek to drain their life, a power so massive, unhearing, and voiceless that it cannot even be called cruel, a power that gives and takes away, lifts up and casts down without appeal.

However it shows itself, sacred power is distinguished from ordinary profane power in that it does not appear as something that man can completely master. He may have some sort of relation to Power—he may enjoy a certain connection with it in religious rite—but religion, properly speaking, is absent whenever the religious object has been reduced to the manipulable and everyday. The sacred always confounds the efforts of practical man to control it. It insists upon itself as the wholly other, refusing to submit to the normal procedures by which man manages his life. Moses hears from the bush, "Put off your shoes . . . for the place on which you are standing is holy ground." This command establishes the boundaries between the religious and the secular, the sacred and the profane.

If a man cannot own, master, or control the sacred, what, then, describes his relationship to it? Luther describes the religious man as clinging or confiding. "I say whatever your heart clings to and confides in, that is really your God."* The phenomenologists of religion have preferred the term "awe" to make it clear that the religious man not only clings to his object with love but also shies away from it in dread. Toward the sacred, he is given to an ambivalent attitude; he neither moves easily toward it nor casually away from it. He is subject to a strange vibration, a motionless motion, like a hummingbird whose wings beat furiously while it hovers in one spot. But even the term awe is handicapped by its associations with developed traditions; it connotes the proper attitude toward a proper god, obscuring that primordial religious attitude that precedes all moral exhortation.

Originally the word religion meant most simply "alertness" or

* Martin Luther, "Exposition of the Ten Commandments," from *The Large Catechism*, as quoted in Waldo Beach and H. Richard Niebuhr, *Christian Ethics* (New York: Ronald Press Co., 1955), p. 245.

"attentiveness."• The sacred always approaches as the fascinating. When it appears, there can be no attending to something else. That is why at the level of cultic routine we use the phrase, "religious observance." There is nothing to do before the sacred except to give it our attention, let it be what it is, let it run its course, and let our own life be caught up in its force.

If men as religious beings deny God, they do not turn their backs on him for nothing; they center their lives in other powers that arrest their attention. This movement away from God is described in two ways in the Old Testament; we are concerned in this chapter with the first, which is called idolatry. When Moses delayed coming down from Mt. Sinai, Aaron spoke to the children of Israel:

> "Take off the rings of gold which are in the ears of your wives, your sons, and your daughters, and bring them to me." . . . And he received the gold at their hand, and fashioned it with a graving tool, and made a molten calf; and they said, "These are your gods, O Israel, who brought you up out of the land of Egypt!" . . . And they rose up early on the morrow and offered burnt offerings and brought peace offerings; and the people sat down to eat and drink, and rose up to play.
>
> Exodus 32:2, 4, 6

Men deny God by turning away from him toward some creaturely power, whether it is the glitter of gold, the fertility of the soil, the excitement of a career, the fascination of a woman, or the claim of a great public cause. Man not only lives in the world, he magnifies the world; he takes something out of its place and glorifies it. He is seldom satisfied to create things with his hands and brains; he must have "miracle" drugs and "wonder" products. It is not enough for him to have friends he enjoys; there must be important people he knows, whose names he can drop in casual conversation. There is a kind of perpetual, cosmic naïveté in the attempt to invest the world with divinity, whether in the enthusiasm of the young who hope that a handful of

---

• See Gerardus van der Leeuw, *Religion in Essence and Manifestation*, trans. J. E. Turner (2 Vols.; New York: Harper & Row, 1963), I, 50; II, 340.

stardust will fall on a weekend meeting, or in the fever of the new man on the job who thrives on the special pressures of the moment. We do not simply live in the world; we strain after deity, hoping that the gods will touch us and that a little of their glamour will brush off in our lives and light up for us the ordinary way.

Traditional interpreters of the sin of idolatry identified particular, discrete objects of devotion in which men center their lives.[*] There are two possible ways of relating to the idol so understood. In polytheism (H. Richard Niebuhr has said that the natural religion of most men is polytheistic), the idol is one of several in a world full of gods. The idolator is free to worship, in varying ways and degrees, a plurality of divine powers. In monolatry, a single idol becomes an exclusive object of devotion, so much so that it no longer exists as one discrete object among others in a more comprehensive environment; it becomes the very principle by which one's world is constituted and organized. Thus the Bitch Goddess Success is never content with a limited place among other allegiances but tends to become "everything" in a man's life. Worship focuses, for all practical purposes, on a single, commanding, and world-organizing power.

There is a third distinct possibility. A man may fall prey, not to a discrete object in a world of objects, or to a single object in and through which his world is organized, but to the world itself. It would be tempting to describe this religious response as pantheistic, except that in contemporary experience it is seldom accompanied by a systematic admiration for the world as divine. This phenomenon, described by the New Testament as bondage to the world,[**] is the most prevalent form of idolatry today.

It is questionable whether the forces that consume and

---

[*] The best sources known to the author on the subject of idolatry are Exodus 32; I Kings 18; II Isaiah 41, 44; Luther's "Exposition of the Ten Commandments," *op. cit.;* Soren Kierkegaard's *Purity of Heart,* trans. Douglas Steere (New York: Harper & Row, 1948); and H. Richard Niebuhr's *Radical Monotheism and Western Culture* (London: Faber & Faber Ltd., 1961).

[**] See Rudolph Bultmann, *Theology of the New Testament* (2 Vols.; New York: Scribner's, 1952), I, 254–258, for commentary on I Corinthians 2:12; 7:32–34; and Romans 8:38.

squander a man's resources can be described as discrete, limited, and identifiable powers. In this respect, the traditional notion of idolatry presumes too much upon a static, stable world, with each idol screwed down in its place and holding court over its own peculiar set of devotees. We live, rather, in a spiritual environment in which powers flicker in and out of the center of attention in a total field of which they are a part. In a particular suburb it is hard to say what a man belongs to. His car, his wife, his time, his colleagues are all caught up in a confusion of impressions, claims, enthusiasms, and disappointments. There is no particular idol among the idols, no precise hierarchy among the gods. Stable distinctions between the sacred and the profane, the exalted and the unfulfilling, are broken down with respect to any given entity, and yet just as surely the idolater is religiously caught up and exhausted by the total world to which he belongs. No art form has recorded this religious thralldom so sensitively as the modern motion-picture camera with its presentation of a world that floods in upon a man as the *only* reality to which he can and ought to devote himself, a world without God.

Captive to and yet responsible for idolatry

The story in Exodus 32 emphasizes the element of bondage to the idol and yet counterbalances it with a sense of responsibility for idolatry.

So far, our interpretation of the sin as a state of religious thralldom has emphasized the aspect of bondage. There are three elements in the story to reinforce it. First, the act of turning away from God takes place while God is not around. He is off on a mountain with Moses, his servant, who delays coming down. The people complain, "We do not know what has become of him." Consequently, there is something believable, natural, and even inevitable about the turn of events. Rallying around the golden calf does not appear to be an act of defiance but rather an automatic adjustment to the absence of one power and the presence of another. Idolatry has this aspect of plausibility also for a Christian, but even more acutely than for the ancient Israelite. If

Moses, the servant of God, delayed coming down from the mountain, how much more has the Son of God delayed in establishing
his kingdom? It seems so much more reasonable to organize life
in the interim around other powers that command the attention.
God is absent, and the god is present, so let the dance around the
golden calf begin.

There is a second reason for man's bondage to idolatry, quite
in additon to the apparent absence of God. The idol also en-
slaves because men feel keenly the threat of the void that would
be theirs without it. The Israelites, after all, find it a little scary
down on the desert floor (and later, it is even scarier among all
those strangers in the land of Canaan). Build the fires and let the
people dance, because without the fire and the dance, night will
fall.

This is the reason for slavery to which modern theologians
such as H. Richard Niebuhr and Paul Tillich have been sensitive. Tillich used the language of the mystic and the romantic
and called it the threat of nonbeing. When men turned away
from the living God and face toward something in this world to
make it their god, they become slaves because their idol stands
between them and the nothing that would be theirs without it. A
person hates to give up a dwindling conversation with his friends
because when they go home his room is vacant. A businessman
fears his retirement because, separated from his career, his life
would be empty. The love song declares, "I can't live without
you because"—as the next line predictably explains—"life without you would be nothing."

Thirdly, although the threat of the void is important to
idolatry, it should not obscure the power of the idol itself to
arrest attention. Our bondage to the idol may result not simply
from the crush of nonbeing that crowds us to the idol's face, but
also from the positive lure of the idol that inspires us to seek its
presence. The song that says "Life without you would be nothing" may not testify to the power of "nothing." It may simply
mean: "My beloved is everything." When a man is a slave to his
job, what difference does it make that his health, his heart, his
time, and his imagination are consumed in its service? His attachment, in this case, is not the push of nonbeing from behind

him but the pull of the idol before him. Nothing else matters.
The golden calf itself may bring the Israelites to their feet and
inspire them to dance.

If for all these varying reasons it can be said that man is in
bondage to his idols, how can it also be said that he is responsible
for idolatry? How is it possible to assert that idolatry is also his
sin? Scripture clearly reckons with it as such. From the very outset of the episode it is obvious that the people are engaged in a
foolishness which they themselves ought to recognize and for
which they are therefore accountable. The gold, after all, comes
from the rings in their very own ears. The idol is the object of
worship and yet it has the stamp of manufacture on it. (See also
Isaiah 44:9–20.) Idolatry is worship, but it is false worship. There
is an element of stupid exaggeration about it from the beginning. A fragment of the creation has been elevated out of its
place. And even when that fragment is not conspicuously a
manufactured object (such as gold rings and corporations) but
the sun, the moon, and the stars, even then there is a recognizable
element of fabrication in the act of idolizing. Every idolator is a
bit of a Wizard of Oz, working the strings from behind the
scenes. Although he is mesmerized by the idol, he is also self-
mesmerizing. Even while saying "I can't help myself," he is preparing for the day when he will say, "What a fool I have been."
As Augustine put it, he sins necessarily and yet he does so will-
ingly.

Idolatry as false worship

A man can be false in two ways: objectively, by falsely evaluat-
ing the object before him; subjectively, by falsifying himself before the object. In both respects, idolatry is false worship.

Idolatry is objectively false in that it elevates a fragment of the
creation into the position of God by conferring upon it the
power and the glory which belong properly to God alone. This
distorts the object not only in its relationship to God but in its
relationships to other elements in the creation and to one's fellow
man. When the idol is singled out for exclusive devotion, either

it occupies an exaggerated position *within* the world or, even worse, it becomes the very principle by which the world is organized. This is the idolator's distortion of the rest of creation. But he also distorts his relationship to his fellow man. Idolatry is inherently divisive. When success is worshiped, it is "my success, not yours." Not that the idol is incapable of establishing community within a circle of adherents, but it tends to thrive on what it excludes. What would the white race be without the black race from which to distinguish itself? It has been said more than once that the idol is the one who is "my god, not yours."

Idolatry is subjectively false in that it also distorts the worshiper before the object. Authentic worship includes the elements of both self-surrender and self-affirmation, that is, self-donation and personal integrity. Martin D'Arcy once referred to these elements as the principles of *anima* and *animus* in the human spirit.* In authentic worship of the true God, man both donates himself wholly and yet is wholly himself. But in idolatry, the authentic element of self-surrender tends to become self-destruction; and the authentic element of self-affirmation tends to become self-expansion. A hidden *Liebestod* prompts me to let myself be burnt up, and burnt out, by my idol. I immolate myself in it. Yet at the same time I borrow prestige from the idol. It is, after all, my god. I expand myself through it.

Impurity of heart

The objective and the subjective aspects of the problem of idolatry are best linked together in the prophetic-priestly term Kierkegaard used in his essay on monotheism: impurity of heart.** Purity of heart is not a sexual term. It refers primarily to singlemindedness, wholeness, integrity, or unity of heart. Impurity of heart, correspondingly, means a heart divided in its allegiances—double-minded, as it were.

The objective basis for purity of heart is monotheism. The

* See M. C. D'Arcy, S.J., *The Mind and Heart of Love* (London: Faber & Faber Ltd., 1954), chap. vii.
** Søren Kierkegaard, *Purity of Heart, op. cit.*

prophets and priests called for purity of heart because God is one—therefore, the heart should be purely his. "Hear, O Israel: the Lord our God is one Lord." This declarative sentence is the objective basis for the negative and positive imperatives: "Thou shalt have no other gods before me," and "Thou shalt love the Lord thy God with all thine heart, and with all thy soul and with all thy might."

Kierkegaard defined the subjective correlate of this monotheism in the simplest of terms, by appeal to the letter of James: "Purify your hearts, you men of double mind" (James 4:8). If the world were composed of a plurality of divine powers, then it would be wrong to love God with wholeness of heart. The heart ought to be shared tactfully with all the good powers that be. Men ought to live appreciatively in relationship to a full host of deities. If God is one, however, then the heart belongs to him alone. In idolatry, the soul forsakes the integrity of its heart before the one God by glutting itself with other powers and glories that vie for its attention. It is guilty of the sin of impurity of heart.

Redemption from sin

Man is both captive and responsible; his idol is both compelling and contrived; this is why the Christian faith has always reckoned with redemption as including both forgiveness and liberation.

First, it clearly requires forgiveness. If man were not responsible for his sin, the act of forgiveness would be gratuitous rather than gracious. Man would need liberation (or sympathy in the absence of liberation) but not mercy directed toward him as a sinner. He would stand in no particular need of inward cleansing. But because man is guilty, because he *consents* to the powers that enthrall him, his redemption is incomplete without forgiveness. Liberation alone would be too external—like a criminal's recovery from a raging fever only to discover that he faces the hopeless snarl of his guilt and the ensuing trial, or like an adulterous husband who has gotten over the affair but whose relations with his wife remain in a state of confusion.

But even more clearly, redemption requires liberation. This liberation takes place only in and through the presence of God, for only in the light of that presence does the idol stand exposed in its powerlessness (I Kings 18:17–46; Isaiah 40–43:20; I Corinthians 8:4–6). It is not the aim of this chapter to elaborate the modes of that presence. Let it be noted simply that the human reflex before God's presence is liberation. His original approach to Moses (Exodus 3) has its consequence in the deliverance of the Israelite people from captivity. His union with man in Jesus of Nazareth means the deliverance of men from the captivity of sin. When the reality of God is established with men the unreality of the idol is exposed.

This event of liberation produces the critical question of faith, and much has been written about it: Shall I cling to God or to the idol? But, in fact, for the man of faith this critical question never presents itself as a choice between symmetrically balanced alternatives. There is something absurdly incomparable about the idol brought up against God. Who can measure the idols of the nations against the Lord of heaven and earth? Academic comparison is utterly impossible and so the Prophets give up the attempt and resort to ridicule (Isaiah 41:7; 44:18–20; I Kings 18:27). For the liberated man the crisis of faith is like the crisis of laughter. The sobering power of the idol is broken up in a guffaw. In the *Treasure of Sierra Madre* a wind sweeps across the desert and blows gold dust away, and men who had surrendered themselves humorlessly, passionately, and murderously to gold, break up in spasms of laughter. So the nomad's word for the Spirit of God is the desert wind, the fiery blast, and, compared with his power, the idol is of no account.

For the Christian, however, the justification for prophetic ridicule is the exposure of God himself to ridicule. God made himself savingly present to men by uniting himself with a man of absolute purity of heart. He presented himself to men only through the medium of that purity of heart to which man himself is summoned. With full human integrity, the Savior surrenders himself

to the will of the Father and suffers ridicule at the hands of
sinners and for the sake of sinners. The ancient taunts of the
Prophets directed against the powerlessness of the idols now come
to roost in taunts directed at the Savior himself. And yet, when
the laughter has died down, a dying Savior, in adoration of the
Father and in solidarity with his brothers, remains. His excruciating presence in human affairs has made the unholy decision of
idolatry itself seem ridiculous. He opens up in the future of all
men the possibility of a holy mirth.

The truth of idolatry

One way of taking idolatry too seriously is to be so wary of it as
to overlook its truth. If the truth of idolatry is neglected, not
only will its power as a sin be underestimated (each sin thrives
on its own special truths) but certain elements in the Christian
life itself will be obscured.

The truth of idolatry is twofold: first, objectively considered,
there is something awesome about the sun, the moon, and the
stars, the cycle of the seasons, the work of genius, and the splendor of the human city; second, as subjectively constituted,
human beings are not insensitive to the world in its variety and
thrall; man is *anima* as well as *animus:* "feminine," receptive,
vulnerable, and surrendering, as well as "masculine," active,
mastering, and self-affirming; there is some truth in the idolator's
recognition of the greatness of the world and the poverty of his
own powers.

From the outset an attempt has been made to reckon with
these truths in the analysis of the power of idolatry, but what can
be said of their place and importance in the Christian life itself?
Is there any place for a celebrational attitude toward the world
and its powers which the Christian ought not deny? This is a
particularly acute problem for the Protestant tradition, since its
theology and worship were formed in massive reaction against
the dangers of idolatry discerned in the Roman Catholic attitude
toward images, saints, and ecclesiastical authority. For the sake of

a singular and exclusive devotion to Christ, the Reformers made an effort to purge Protestant worship and life of every trace of sin.

This was not originally an objectionable development. Despite their attack on idolatry, Luther and Calvin maintained a fine sense of the splendor of the world. But often Protestant preaching has sought to honor Christ by dishonoring the world. The end result is to distract from Christ by concentrating on the task of devaluing the world. At length, Christ himself is defied. He redeemed the world not by undoing creation but by entering into it. To render to such a redeemer his just due is to cherish him in the very world he entered. There is an untruth in worship whose fervor depends entirely upon a flattening out of man and his world, as though God will stand out in full color and splendor only if the world and man are penciled gray.

Etienne Gilson has argued that to do justice to the world one must do justice to God.* The objective basis for doing justice to the world is the obdurate worth, power, and valency of created things; but the subjective condition for doing justice to the world is a recognition of the importance of *anima* as well as *animus* in man's contact with the world. Only insofar as a man remains fully sensitive, open, receptive, and, indeed, vulnerable to his environment does he reckon with it in its full diversity and splendor.

In respect to this subjective element, Protestantism has faced its difficulties. It has espoused, as its ideal for man's relationship to the world, the principle of *animus* alone. The elements of *anima* in the psychic life were subordinated to the tasks of self-control and world-conquest. It sent out into the world a man of destiny, self-affirming and world-mastering, who carved up a universe desacralized. In this sense, there has been a deep affinity between Protestantism and the emergence of the ideals of a secular civilization.

There is no reason to criticize the human struggle for self-affirmation and mastery. (Our chapter on avarice will attempt to

* See Etienne Gilson, *The Spirit of Medieval Philosophy*, trans. A. H. C. Downes (London: Sheed & Ward, 1950), pp. 144–145.

reckon with the importance of this struggle.) But as an obsessive cultural ideal it obscures the sensitive factors in human existence through which the world in its full diversity and delectability makes itself known. It produces what Weber called a thisworldly asceticism—lean, spare, joyless, wraithlike, and male. It produces the comedy of a man who makes a million dollars but who is psychically incapable of enjoying it. And it produces one final, delicious irony. Even though it desacralizes the universe and defeminizes the human spirit, it manages in its own peculiar way to reintroduce them both. While condemning the mother goddess of Roman Catholicism, it substitutes for her the Bitch Goddess Success.

2 False Fear: The Sin Of FAINTHEARTEDNESS

The religious rejection of God is usually described within the general framework of the preceding chapter. Richard Niebuhr is typical on the subject when he observes that the natural religion of most men is polytheism. Men desert God by streaking their world with deity. They flee from him by becoming informal polytheists or pantheists, attempting to pull their life from their sensuality, their sophistication, or their ambition in turn. This is the atheism of impurity of heart.

But there is a second way in which men deny God religiously. They reject him not only when they turn to some positive good or power which they find enthralling, but also when they turn to some evil, danger, or worry that lies ahead and find it overwhelming. This is what might be called the atheism of the *fainthearted.*

Usually no one recognizes faintheartedness as a denial of God. It is easy to see that a man rejects God when, like a robust pagan, he substitutes other gods in his place. It is more difficult to recognize when he becomes fainthearted before powers that menace and threaten him, especially because he is inclined under these circumstances to dissolve in self-pity.

Yet this is the most dominant form of the denial of God today. The gods that enthrall men are not powers that bless but those that threaten. We do not think of evils as controllable, but rather as encompassing powers that we can barely touch or affect. We are content simply to watch them with fascination. Today we are not so much polytheists or pantheists who defy the world; we are (it is difficult to summarize the varieties of this religious mood with a single word) demonists, fatalists, or Manichaean pessimists who believe that the world and its future are in the grasp of destructive, voiceless, and unhearing power.

In the last chapter religion was defined simply as "alertness" or "attentiveness." A man's religion is whatever he attends to with his whole being. Defined this way, the "natural religion" of most men today is not ordinarily one of the traditional gods. Toward his sexuality, ambition, the state, and so forth, the modern person has learned how to "play it cool." In their place he attends to destructive power, fate, and death.

This religious preoccupation is clearly in evidence in the daily newspaper, which is almost entirely devoted to telling us what death, murder, crime, corruption, fire, and panic have accomplished in the past twenty-four hours.* We so accept this peculiar preoccuption that we are inclined to forget that the papers might conceivably focus on something else—on lectures, stories of community co-operation, and the biographies of inspiring men. But, of course, they do not, because these newspapers would not sell. Their "news" simply would not command attention. Only evils that have had an explosive impact in the last few hours have sufficient energy, vitality, and lure to make the headlines.

In fact, we live in an age when every instrument of mass media

---

* Karl Barth has recommended that Christians scrutinize well both the Bible and the newspaper. Arthur C. McGill has lectured forcefully on the religious preoccupations of the front page: "Demonism: the Spiritual Reality of Our Age" (Harvard Divinity School, Spring, 1966).

is consecrated to the menacing and the threatening. No one can listen to a modern news broadcaster assemble his list of disasters from every corner of the globe, or watch a panel of reporters draw blood from a political leader on a television interview without realizing that modern instruments of mass media have their own natural sense of consummation in their work as harbingers of the threatening. Not even the most buoyant of our magazines, the *Reader's Digest,* with its choppy, cheerful sentences can get along a single month without reporting on such matters as cholestrol counts or cancer.

Mass media, of course, not only report violence but also become its producers. The sheer act of bringing certain events into the public domain and maintaining them there at the center of attention has a way of magnifying their explosive charge. Moreover, the very speed with which they are reported encourages the violent build-up of action, reaction, and collision between all parties involved. No interval of time occurs to cool or to blur the religious impact of events. The news services, as Marshall McLuhan has observed, are for the most part "hot" media. Not only do they report on fires, but the reporting itself is incendiary. This has little to do with the private intentions of particular reporters; rather, it is a consequence of the electricity with which the entire apparatus is charged, in the course of giving people the news that they want.

This zest for violence on the public scene is not itself an expression of faintheartedness. As a matter of fact one of its functions may be to provide people with kicks that will extricate them from their own private worries and humdrum routines. There is something exhilarating about a good fire. It takes the mind off the insuperable sameness of one's everyday problems. Personal faintheartedness may find relief in, rather than result from, our obsession with violence in the public domain. If this is true, then we have not yet arrived at that special form of the experience of destructive power which provides the setting for the sin.

Demonism and Manichaean dualism

When destructive powers are experienced as plural, profuse, explosive, and perhaps even exhilarating, the best term for characterizing the experience is demonism. When destructive forces are reduced to a single, satanic power, then Manichaean (or Marcionite) dualism best characterizes the religious experience involved.

The early Manichees were metaphysical dualists who insisted on a radical distinction between Light and Darkness, Good and Evil, Spirit and Matter. On the basis of this distinction, they were also advocates of the ascetic life, rejecting marriage, property, and children. These secondary features of Manichaeism need not concern us here. More important is the fundamental mood of pessimism by which it was controlled. For a Manichaean (in any age) the world is fundamentally irredeemable—gripped as it is in the hands of comprehensive and destructive power. In our own time, the Manichaean response to a threatened world takes one of three forms: active-heroic, paranoidal, and passive-philistine. Each exhibits its own distinctive attitude toward a threatened world, ranging from the courageous, to the malicious, to the fainthearted.

The active-heroic response to a threatened world is a little closer to the spirit and views of the ancient Marcionites than the Manichaeans. The Marcionites distinguished between two gods—the creator god of power and the redeemer god of love. Modern Marcionites no longer subscribe to a redeemer-god of love, but they do distinguish between two realms: a *transcendental* order of destructive power ("the whole world is organized by death," says one of the heroes of Camus's *The Plague*) and a *human* order of love. The Myth of Sisyphus symbolized for Camus the plight of man. The relatively innocent victim of a harsh cosmos, Sisyphus is forced to carry a stone ceaselessly and meaninglessly to the top of a hill only to have it roll down again. He stands for man under sentence of death in an irredeemable world. His only authentic response to his plight is resolute, lucid, and unavailing protest against his lot. The existence of this type of literature warns the theologian not to make a cheap appeal to the Christian faith as the only "courageous" solution to the problem of destructive power in our time.

The paranoidal version of Manichaean dualism today is found especially in the political ideology of the Right and Left. Both impute a satanic strength and malevolence to their rivals. The pluralist world of the demonist is simplified as the demons are reduced to one: Communism, the Jew, or the Black Race; or, alternatively, Capitalism, the Roman Catholic Hierarchy, or perhaps the WASP.

In this case, once again, the spiritual problem is not faintheartedness (the political dualist, after all, is capable of an aggressive, military sort of courage); the more serious spiritual problem is malice (and, because this is the case, it will be explored more fully in the chapter on hatred).

This leaves, then, one remaining form of dualism as the basis for faintheartedness—a somewhat more self-pitying Manichaean gloom which we have called passive-philistine. Its hero is not the resolute figure of protest literature or the venomous zealot from the radical Right or Left but rather the little fellow struggling under the pressures of a big world, for whom defiance of the world is out of the question; he seeks only a limited sanctuary from its blows.

The story of the non-hero is repeated endlessly in TV and movie plots; one example should suffice. In the movie version of Nelson Algren's *The Man With the Golden Arm,* Frank Sinatra plays the part of a dope addict, Frankie Machine, who is the frightened victim of Chicago's Near North Side, a nagging wife who had tricked him into marriage, the gambler Schwiefka, and the dope peddler Louis. But he is comforted by the understanding of his mistress, Molly-O, played by Kim Novak, who, in one of the most impressive displays of privileged sanctuary, covers him as he lies shivering on the floor, with a coat and her own body.

Somewhat less spectacularly, each man in his own way seeks his Molly-O, a sanctuary in a world he finds unfulfilling. He seeks from a redeemer figure not forgiveness but a little bit of sympathy, understanding, and pity. This is the mood out of which the specific sin of faintheartedness emerges. A man denies God because, for all practical purposes, his life is a lonely struggle between himself and the job that seems too much, the illness that discourages, or the excitement that always appears to happen to someone else. Or again, he is tempted to faintheartedness as he lies in bed at night worrying about the coming days as though life were a solitary struggle between his own pitiful resources and the monstrous obligations that fill the morrow.

Parents and the Grand Inquisitor

Men can be fainthearted not only by the timidity with which they handle their own problems, but also in the apprehensive way in which they handle the problems of others. This is particularly true in the case of the negligent parent who is so absorbed in himself and his own career that he forgets his children; but it is just as true of the parent who is so worried that he believes there are only two realities: his love for his child, and the suffering from which he wants to protect him. Such love is impressive in its own way, but such a parent operates as though God could not possibly do anything in and through the suffering of his children.

The modern conscientious parent, in fact, occupies the religious position of Dostoevski's Grand Inquisitor, whose symbolic role was explained as being motivated by his passionate love for men and the grim suffering from which he desired to protect them. Men of conscience in positions of responsibility are particularly tempted to reject God and become saviors in their own right. And, of course, because they cannot do a very good job of it, they are filled with apprehension. What an anomaly it must be for a child to see his parents go to a Christian church and yet betray, by the worry written across their faces, their great secret fear that God is dead!

Finally, there is today a special form of faintheartedness to-

ward the future that afflicts the young; those who shy away from
the future, who stall nervously on the question of the scope of
their talents, and who are afraid to leave the gods of youth and
their sheltering securities and press across the frontier into their
own maturity. These young people are especially likely to be
given to faintheartedness about the future, for our society does
not help its young across the frontier into adult life. This is
particularly obvious in the contrast between the ways in which
primitive and modern young people are called upon to make
their way into adult life.

In a primitive society there is a single, decisive, dramatic, even
bloody rite to mark the transition from childhood to adult life—
isolation in a hut, a whipping, a tattooing, or even the pulling of
a tooth. (In more civilized societies, by contrast, we have
gentle rites: orientation weeks and unalarming commencement
exercises.) Whatever may be the rigors of his ancient rites, the
primitive has one important advantage. He goes into the rite a
child, is stamped, and comes out the other side an adult ready to
assume both the privileges and responsibilities of life in the
human tribe.

But instead of a single great crashing stroke through one's life
at the age of sixteen, we have all sorts of little strokes that intersect a man's life anywhere from fourteen to forty-three, marking
his transition to the adult world. He does not travel quickly
and dramatically from one country into another. He enters into
a no man's land with all sorts of swift turns and subtle experiences, elusive longings and anxieties which are hard to subdue.
In the course of this journey he is tempted to faintheartedness.
He is beset by private worries about talent, uncertainty as to his
identity in the eyes of his parents and peers, and strange appre-
hensions about the future that simply would not occur to the
primitive.

Not that the community does nothing for men today. All are
its debtors in countless ways. But none of those gifts received
from the community is able to stamp the young with an adult
life. In effect, each has to learn how to cross the frontier into
adulthood alone.

Fear, fearlessness, true fear, and false fear

In the cultural analysis offered so far, no clear distinction has been made between fear as a psychic fact and the sin of faintheartedness. The natural emotion of fear may be the occasion for faintheartedness, but it is not itself the sin. Distinctions are necessary between four phenomena: fear as a psychic fact, fearlessness, true fear, and false fear.

First, fear as a psychic fact is a simple recoil before an object that threatens. This experience, far from being a sin, may point truthfully both to the goodness of creation and to the limitations on human powers. Natural fear presupposes the goodness of creation, because it testifies to the worth of certain objects which are threatened with destruction. Only the religious traditions of the East with their ethic of detachment propose fearlessness as a religious ideal. Since the world of desirable goods itself is denied, no attachments remain to be threatened. Natural fear is overcome in a state of psychic anesthesia. The only other way in which fearlessness can be proposed as an ideal occurs in fantasy rather than religion. In the Superman comics of the West a child soars above the problem of courage into the daydream world of unlimited powers and fearlessness. The biblical tradition, on the contrary, recognizes fear as a psychic fact; it does not require a man to ignore real threats (either to himself or to his children) for what they are. His courage depends not on the dissolution of the realm of threat, but upon the recognition that none can threaten him ultimately; no giant problem, no evil day, and no fortified city can separate him from God's power.

Second, true fear, in the theological sense, is different from a simple recoil before a threatening object. The fear of the Lord which is the beginning of wisdom (and courage) is that state in which a human being is rooted or anchored in the life of God.*

* Blessed is the man who fears the Lord,

.   .   .   .

He is not afraid of evil tidings;
  his heart is firm, trusting in the Lord.
His heart is steady, he will not be afraid. . . .
                              Psalm 112:1, 7, 8a

The objective basis for this fear, as Psalm 96 makes clear, is the acknowledgment of God as the Lord of glory. The glory of God refers, among other things, to the wealth of God's life, his weight and substance. God is to be feared, not because he is the transcendent Lord who dwells far above men, but because he is weightier, more substantial, than all other beings. A life rooted in him becomes the constraining principle of activity in relationship to all other powers. While not excluding the experience of recoil (Gethsemane is evidence for it), the fear of God permits one to live with his fears without letting their objects become the very principle of his life.

False fear, correspondingly, is the refusal to accept God as the weightiest thing in one's life. Other powers seem weightier: perhaps the judgment of a boss to whom a man obsequiously defers, the opinions of his peer group by which he is intimidated, or a cloud of obligations that hangs heavy over the future. Faintheartedness goes beyond the simple act of recoil; it is a sinking deference to trouble. In false fear, a man roots his being in a threatening power from which he takes his entire bearings—whether it be the satanic energies of his enemies or simply the heavy burdens imposed upon him by a big world. That is why we have resorted to the language of religion to describe the state of a man in its throes.

If these definitions are correct, Christian courage cannot be defined as a state of fearlessness or weightlessness. Rather it poses the question: whom shall I fear? Shall I fear the judgments of others, the bad news of the doctor, the uncertainties of the new job, the possibility of my failure; or shall I fear the Lord?* My fear of the Lord, in turn, cannot be based on his possession of an all-sovereign competence by virtue of which he rescues me from trouble. Such a God, perhaps externally helpful in overcoming one crisis or another, is not one in whose substance human courage might be inwardly nourished.

The Christian basis for courage is the discovery that God is not an aloof, self-sufficient, and impenetrable deity into whose life roots could not extend. The son of God himself has received—

* See Psalms 46 and 112.

and rooted—his life wholly in the Father. There is a place in the divine life itself for true fear; Jesus met it in the very arena where men know the pressures of natural, and the distortions of unnatural, fear. Christian courage, therefore, does not wait for a celestial superman to dissolve every threatening power. Jesus does not fly over the human city; he has entered into it and into its innermost fears, and there he has made it known that there is a fortress, a rock, a citadel of true fear in the life of God himself against which all the false fears of men shall not prevail.

Israel in a no man's land

If Exodus 32 is the *locus classicus* on impurity of heart, the first chapter of Deuteronomy is its symmetrical counterpart on faintheartedness. It records a crisis in courage similar to the permanent crisis of men in a no man's land.

Deuteronomy reports that the people of Israel had traveled over a great and terrible wilderness and finally camped across from the hill country of the Amorites which God had promised to them. Moses speaks to his people, saying: " 'Behold, the Lord your God has set the land before you; go up, take possession, as the Lord, the God of your fathers, has told you; do not fear or be dismayed' " (Deuteronomy 1.21).

But then the people get cagey. They propose to send spies into the land of the Amorites, not because they are afraid, but simply so that the scouts " 'may explore the land for us, and bring us word again of the way by which we must go up. . . .' " The spies were sent and brought fruit back with them, saying: " 'It is a good land which the Lord our God gives us.' " Yet still the people would not go into the land. For the scouts of the Israelites had also reported back: " 'The people are greater and taller than we; the cities are great and fortified up to heaven. . . .' " (Deuteronomy 1:22, 25, 28)

On the edge of the promised land, at the very border of the future, the Israelites draw back, sick with apprehension. They think of the future as filled only with themselves and their pathetic resources, pitted against giants that lie in wait to ambush them.

The story expresses that strange ambivalence which everyone feels toward his future: there is fruit in the country ahead, but there are also giants in the land. Moses' reaction to this ambivalent situation is worthy of note. He does not handle his people the way men like to see themselves handled when they are given to inferiority feelings. He does not compliment them. He avoids saying, you are taller than you think you are, brighter and shrewder than the Amorites, more clever than your fathers. Nor does he try to suppress the difficulties that lie ahead. Rather, in the name of Jehovah, he summons his people across this frontier: " 'The Lord your God who goes before you will himself fight for you, just as he did for you in Egypt before your eyes, and in the wilderness, where you have seen how the Lord your God bore you, as a man bears his son, in all the way that you went until you came to this place' " (Deuteronomy 1:30–31). When the Israelites again refuse, then God becomes angry, for in being fainthearted about tomorrow they deny the God who has brought them to the very place where they stand.

Nor does the story end there; for, according to biblical narrative, the children of Israel eventually enter into the land of Canaan. God brings them across this frontier, just as earlier he carried them out of Egypt and bore them across the wilderness. And what God did once for the Israelites, he has extended to all the children of men in the person of his son who crossed the frontier which no one dares to cross. Jesus carried sleepy disciples along with him to Gethsemane, and shouldered the judgment of God on a cross, and went down into his grave, making of that harrowing boundary an entrance into the promised land. Moses invites the Israelites to occupy the land that lies ahead with boldness rather than faintheartedness, saying in effect: "Fear not, neither be dismayed. Behold, Jehovah thy God hath set the land before thee. Go. Take possession of it."

The promised land

This interpretation of the Deuteronomic narrative might be sentimentally misinterpreted as promising God's help in the achievement of any and all goals that a man may choose to pursue. On what grounds should men expect God's aid in the pursuit of their middle-class ideals (a nice Chicago suburb for Frankie Machine, or good grades, success in a job, a suitable wife, and promising children for the rest of us)? Indeed, the frantic pursuit of some of these projects may be idolatrous in itself. There is no reason to suppose that men are invited to substitute for God's own promised land the land of the golden calf and then to expect God's help in obtaining the latter. The first chapter of Deuteronomy ought not to be read apart from Exodus 32.

When it is God's own project about which men are fainthearted, then indeed it is a sin, but fear in the pursuit of some of our own goals may be a natural psychic fact—and gracious signal—rather than a sin. Fear, in these cases, may prompt a truthful recognition of our inability to impose and realize our goals; or again, it may expose the element of idolatry in our relationship to our goals. Thus, God may be the one intimidating us and showing us our poverty; and the recoil of fear, in these instances, may be the cutting edge of grace. Faintheartedness, as a sin, must refer more directly to our refusal to enter into the land that God has promised rather than to our hesitation in entering the lands that we have promised to ourselves.

Some reflection clearly is necessary on the meaning of the "promised land" for the Christian; for obviously it has meant a variety of goals for different groups. For positive thinkers it has been identified with a middle-class success; for depressed races or classes, with their promotion to the next social level or, even more radically, it has referred to that delicious revolutionary moment when the scales themselves are reversed; for the Puritans it meant New England, and for the frontier church, the West—

both of which territories were occupied at bloody expense to the "Amorites" already residing therein.

These various interpretations of the promised land—despite the sentiment they have commanded—put men back behind the event in which the promise of God was fulfilled. For the Christian, God's promise of a land, a temple, and a king to the people of Israel was but a preparatory stage of his own immanent presence in their midst. Jesus himself is the event in which the promises of God are fulfilled. He, is the terrain, temple, and king, if you will, in which men may encounter God in his own person.

This interpretation, of course, immediately raises the question: has there taken place, in the transition from the Old Testament to the New Testament, a ghostly spiritualization of the meaning of the promised land? God's promise to the Jews, after all, was earthy. He promised them a specific land—Canaan—and he made this promise in the teeth of a specific foe—the Amorites. Is the fulfillment of this promise in the New Testament a spiritual sleight of hand, with no power whatsoever to command human fears? Not as the Christian understands it: God—far from realizing his promise in a spiritually vaporous way—actually gave it a living fulfillment. Jesus Christ is not a spiritual volatilization of Jewish hope, but rather its further concretization, as God makes the human terrain itself his habitation. The son of God exposes himself to all the terrors that men face on earth in his passage toward his own death. Thus the man of faith is not provided with an easily shattered ideology, or a fragile "spiritual point of view" on his own terrifying experiences of destructive power, but rather with a specific event of God's love in the flesh, an event as concrete as the Israelite takeover of Canaan or the Puritan takeover of the new world.

The New Testament equivalent for Moses' speech summoning his people to courage is found in the Letter to the Romans. Paul testifies that "neither death, nor life, nor angels, nor principalities, nor things present, nor things to come, nor powers . . . nor anything else in all creation, will be able to separate us from the love of God in Christ Jesus our Lord." Just as the Jews were offered the assurance that nothing could prevent their establishment in the land of Canaan, men have been told that nothing can prevent their establishment in the love of God—neither their own sin and shortcomings nor threats of demons, fate, or death.

But has the meaning of the promised land been so restricted to God's presence in Christ that it no longer has a real connection with man's daily projects and fears, with the problems that face the adolescent, the parent, and the widow? Clearly the connection between the two has lapsed if God must be cast in the role of a supernatural Clark Kent responsible for the dissolution of every difficulty that Metropolis faces. The passage in Romans does not suggest that men experience in this life the dissolution and disappearance of the powers of sin, death, and external threat. Crimes are committed, cancers may grow, and hearts may fail. But the passage does report that these events have been robbed of their ultimacy and exposed in their impotence. Against the ingenerate love of God they shall not prevail.

As a sign of this love, the Christian is called upon to face his own giant problems and fortified cities with a certain measure of Christian calm. He cannot claim that his faith is the only basis for human courage. Stoicism, from Epictetus to Camus, is proof that it is not. But his stoutheartedness in the face of disaster or, even more difficult, in the face of the *possibility* of disaster allows him to offer a sign of that love against which not even faintheartedness, ultimately, will prevail.

3 False Mastery:
AVARICE

The association of certain sins with different members or conditions of the human body is often partly functional and partly metaphorical. Lying is associated with the tongue; envy with the intense gaze of the eyes; lust with the genitals; gluttony with the

throat and stomach (the Latin *gluttus* is the word for throat);
anger with boiling blood; pride variously with the puffed chest
or the heart; conceit with the turned head; condescension and
curiosity, in their different ways, with the nose; and, finally,
avarice, with the arms and hands.

In Molière's play *L'Avare*, the avaricious hero is called
"Harpagon." Appropriately, the name refers to the Greek *harpe*,
which means "claw" or "sickle." The avaricious Harpagon, in
effect, is a grappling hook, a vicious extension of the human
arm and hand. Something of the same range of metaphor is
present in the classical biblical passage on avarice: "For the love
of money is the root of all evils; it is through this craving that
some have wandered away from the faith. . . ." (Timothy 6:10)
The Greek word for craving in this passage is a form of *oregomai*,
which means literally to "extend the arms after." Avarice is a
reaching and a grasping. The Apostle Paul makes use of the
metaphor (by way of negation) as he describes the coming of the
Savior, who, "though he was in the form of God, did not count
equality with God a thing to be grasped. . . ." (Philippians 2:6)
The covetous man on the contrary, lays his hands on anything he
can get. He may even snatch away the goods of another. And
after he gets them, he clutches them. He is often called tight-
fisted. Our metaphors for avarice rely inevitably on the arms and
the hands.

Avarice has often been defined in the classical theological
tradition as an inordinate love of possessing. The simplest verb
for the expression of ownership is the verb "to have." Consequently the term for avarice in many languages is affiliated with
the word for having, which is naturally related to the arms and
the hands. Things come into our possession by our reaching for
them. Once they become ours, we attempt to exercise a certain
control over them, a mastery, which is best expressed by the
hands. Our possessions are our "holdings."

The primacy of this element of possession and control distinguishes avarice from idolatry. Clearly the two sins may overlap.
There is a strong element of idolatry in avarice. The miser makes
a god of his money in the sense that it defines his life. But in

idolatry the element of immolation and surrender to the object adored is primary, the element of ownership and control secondary; whereas in avarice, the priorities are reversed. Avarice is masculine rather than feminine. The miser does not give himself to an object in the manner of a woman; he wants to hold it in his hands like a man.

This distinction between idolatry and avarice can be put in another way. The sins considered so far—idolatry and faintheartedness—are both sins of the religious man, whereas avarice is peculiarly the sin of the secular, or profane, man. The religious realm is precisely that realm in which man does not feel himself to be in charge. There he encounters power which is overmastering, incalculable, and mysterious. His control, at best, is minimal and circumspect. The profane realm, however, is precisely the workaday world in which man exercises lordship and mastery. In this domain, as much as possible is reduced to measure, calculation, security, and control. Seen in this light, idolatry and faintheartedness are religious sins; avarice, secular sin. The idolatrous and the fainthearted man come under the thrall of a power (good or evil) to which they yield themselves in the place of God. In this sense, both sins are religious and feminine. Avarice, however, is not primarily a yielding; it is an acquiring and controlling. It is masculine and profane. Quite appropriately, therefore, it has been the besetting sin of the modern bourgeois—that most striking hero of an emergent secular civilization—whose chief aim in life has been ownership, mastery, and control.

Conceived in this way, the sin of avarice deserves a broader definition than that accepted by Thomas Aquinas. The medieval theologian took advantage of the literal meaning of one of the words for avarice in the New Testament (*philarguros,* lover of silver) to restrict the term to the inordinate love of money. The very power of money, however, is such as to point the way to a broader definition. St. Thomas justified the statement that money is the root of all evil in noting that it is man's usual and pre-eminent means to the possession of all other things. Conceived more broadly, therefore, the sin of avarice refers to false possession and mastery—whether exercised over money, other external objects, one's neighbor, or even over one's self, in defiance of God. The key word in this definition is "false." It implies that there is such a thing as a responsible order of possession and mastery before God. What this order is must be suggested in each case, but in all cases, false mastery involves a defiance of God. This defiance is implicit in the theological expression with which money itself is tagged: "the almighty dollar."

Covetousness and things

Although the definition of avarice must be broadened to include the full spectrum of sins in the order of having, the first in this spectrum is avarice as directed to external objects rather than persons. "You shall not covet your neighbor's house" (Exodus 20:17). The Bible also warns that you shall not covet your neighbor's wife. But, in fact, a man usually does not. Despite the lavish attention paid to this form of covetousness in novels, a man is generally content to covet his neighbor's job or his money.

The desire for possessions may be quantitative or qualitative in character. Hoarding is usually quantitative. Money is a chief object of avarice, not only because it provides the means for the control of many other objects, but also because it offers the very simple satisfaction that it can be counted.* The covetous man enjoys an increment to his own being as the assets pile up. But there is also a certain qualitative sophistication in avarice, according to which the test is not how much, but what, one owns. Here the center of interest is not the bank account or the gold reserves, but, rather, the things that go with suburban upper-middle-class life. Since it does not always take an impossible amount of money in our society to manage such an existence, avarice is not a sin restricted to the rich or to the eccentric. It tempts the modestly provided as well.

* Again, one of the variety of Greek words for avarice is constructed from the word *pleon*, which means "more."

Under conditions of scarcity, avarice usually takes the form of hoarding. Economists have politely described this phenomenon on a widespread scale as the "acquisitive phase" of a society. The symbol of control and possession in such a society is the key. It is a kind of absentee hand, a way of holding on to something while one is elsewhere. In some sections of Europe the key still remains an important mystery in daily life. Keys for cupboards, chests, doors, gates, and drawers abound. They are handed over to children only with the greatest of ceremony or perhaps even reserved for the time of passage into adult life. Keys are natural to a society in which the walls are thick, fences are high, and the proof of ownership and control lies in transporting objects from without to within.

It would be a mistake, however, to identify such a society— retentive and anal as it is—with the dynamic phases of industrial capitalism. The later development of industrial capitalism by the middle class required not only the retention of wealth but also its massive expenditure at critical points for the further development of industry. In this respect, capitalism has been somewhat closer to the phallic than the anal personality of Freudian lore. Hoarding wealth is subordinate to producing it, and producing it, if need be, by a brutal expenditure of energy. Increasingly, the proof of ownership and control shifts to a shrewd expenditure of power through which power itself is produced.

This emphasis on expenditure in industrial capitalism continues with the still later development of an affluent, consumer-oriented society. Expenditure replaces retentiveness as proof of ownership and control. Today in America, and perhaps increasingly elsewhere in the world, the hoarder has been reduced to the position of an eccentric. In an increasingly affluent society, the pleasure and proof of possessions does not lie in transporting them to a darkened room and locking a door, but rather in bringing them out into the open, exhibiting them, and using them up, not modestly, restrictively, discreetly, but conspicuously and without restraint. Picture windows, rather than keys, are proof of what we own. Although Americans may lock their cars for prudential reasons, this act is not a significant sign of ownership. Far more important is the fact that they can buy a car one year, let its rocker panels rust out, and replace it the next.

Economists have described this shift in the sense of ownership in the phrase "conspicuous consumption." We have moved from a society of locks and thick-walled castles, vaults, and secret treasures, to a society of the open door, neon lights, and the picture window, with grain spilling out of silos, cars pouring out of factories, and paper glutting garbage cans. This is a society that no longer hoards—it burns. It burns up money, alcohol, raw materials, and natural resources, and it produces everywhere a stepped-up tempo. Instead of keys, we have keyed-up nerves. Too much drink, too much conversation in overcrowded rooms, a calendar jammed with obligations, phones ringing, overheated homes. The American experience of avarice is not like the anal experience of the recent European past, for which gold and dung, the images of inert weight, are appropriate. We should speak of avarice now rather as a veritable firestorm of activity, generated by flickering, formless desires, and fears that leave a person burnt out and exhausted at the age of fifty. Avarice under the conditions of scarcity means hoarding; under the conditions of abundance it means fiery destruction.

And yet in either case a man seeks to solve the question of his existence by ownership, whether he expresses this absolute right of disposition by placing his goods in dead storage or by burning them up in a sixteen-hour-a-day conflagration.

Possession and control have undergone one further change in modern times. The fact of ownership has become less important than the fact of control. Indeed, the modern managers of capital and resources have emerged as more important and prestigious than the owners themselves. The relation of the manager to resources is still one of the "hands," although the metaphor now suffers an important change in connotation. Instead of "holdings" (a term appropriate to the relatively permanent and stable relationship of an owner to a thing), we speak now of "handling" affairs, "manipulating" the market, or "managing" resources. These words are all derived from terms for the hands, but they now suggest a much more ephemeral, external, remote, and incidental relationship of agent to thing. This fact marks, if any-thing, a further secularization of the sin. In ownership there was a certain religious element. The hoarder took his pleasure in owning, to be sure, but he was also capable of appreciating, if not idolizing, the objects he owned. There was, if you will, a certain contemplative or adorational element in his hoarding. The relationship of the manager to the things he controls, how-ever, is far more incidental. Meaning for him is reserved more strictly for the experience of mastery. In turn, the very virtuosity of his mastery tends to devalue the object in his eyes. The art of managing becomes everything, and the objects managed are thoroughly profaned. Thus, low-key cynicism becomes his most spiritually tolerable style.

It would be wrong, in the foregoing, to interpret all ownership and control of external objects as sinful. This is what certain romanticists have done. They have rejected, on principle, the emergence of secular man. They prefer a legendary, Arcadian past that precedes man's ownership and control of nature. In-stead of limiting avarice to one of the special sins of the secular man, they would reject the secular order in its entirety as evil. Insofar as these romanticists are realists, of course, they concede that the very conditions of creaturely existence are such as to demand a human mastery of nature. Nevertheless, while recog-nizing this fact, they tend to bemoan it. For them, ownership and control are both necessary and evil. Creaturely existence and primordial avarice are hopelessly intertwined.

Avarice, however, is false mastery and not mastery as such. Christian analysis of avarice demands a clear distinction between ownership and control in the contexts of creation and sin. When the two are confused, an improper understanding of each results. Ownership and control are not properly acknowledged as posi-tive ingredients in man's responsible life before God; they are reduced to the melancholic details of creaturely life. Avarice is no longer a sin; it becomes a birthmark, a nuisance, a tragic fate.

According to Genesis, man is placed in the garden of Eden as its caretaker and lord. This position is conditional upon his accountable, responsible life with his companion before God. In the New Testament, too, a positive place is given to man as lord and ruler—especially in the figure of the steward who is charged with responsibility for his master's house. The Old and New Testaments show no particular disposition to favor the quiescent as opposed to the mastering modes of relation to the world. In this respect the current enthusiasm for the "secular man" in theological circles is a corrective to any interpretation of the Gospel, in which all ownership and control are reduced to the profane.

At the same time, however, the place of ownership and control is clearly limited. This limitation is not simply "external" in the sense that man is limited by the double presence of God and the neighbor, to whom and with whom he is responsible. The limitation is inherent in that very power by which he exercises mastery: the power of spirit in unity with the flesh. What particularly interests us here is the flesh.

When the theological tradition has sought to account for man's privileged position of mastery in the cosmos, it has usually done so by pointing to his reason and will. This spiritual endowment, it is argued, distinguishes man as the lord of all other natural beings. Often overlooked in the theological tradition is the further fact that this placement is no less dependent upon man's life in the flesh. Were man a spirit alone, he would neither need, nor have the capacity, to rule the earth. In the absence of the body, there would be nothing to feed and nothing with which to do the feeding. Man would be restricted to ghostly observation alone. Ownership and control are just as dependent upon man's life in the flesh as upon his spiritual powers. Man is caretaker and lord only with the help of his hands. Therefore, when man fails to act as caretaker and lord, he fails to use not only his powers of spirit but his powers of flesh as well.

This dependence of human mastery upon the flesh simultaneously establishes certain limits to the positive meaning of man's dominion over nature. For the flesh has two further meanings for man beyond that of instrument to the mastery of his environment. First, man's flesh renders him acutely vulnerable and open to the creation that falls beyond his rule. The creation is not simply the property owned, the body mastered, and the tools controlled; it is also the wave of heat, the flash of rain, the brilliance of sunshine, the drag of exhaustion, and the shocks of disease and love. These events in their own full-bodied impact on the human spirit are just as much a part of the creation as those that fall under the partial sway of man's control. It is this range of experience from which the man of avarice seeks to shut himself off. Therefore, insofar as he reduces his life to ownership and control alone, he suffers from occlusion—not only the miser's occlusion from the neighbor, important as that is, but also a withdrawal from the creation as a whole. The avaricious man, intent on ownership and control alone, organizes the world exhaustively and tediously in terms of its help and hindrance to that control. To the impoverishment of his own life, he locks himself off from all else.

Seen in this light, avarice cannot be accurately understood as a "materialistic sin"—the rubric under which it is usually classified. In fact, avarice is a withdrawal from the flesh even more profoundly than a removal from the spirit. After all, flesh is the arena where the world we do not and cannot control touches and moves us. The man who withdraws into avarice would like to remove himself from the sudden intrusion of a wonderful disarray of experience—from flash floods to bag-worms, from shapely legs to misshapen shadows at the end of a day. Avarice is one of the coldest of the sins of the spirit. A man withdraws from that fully sensitive encounter with the world which is his only through his vulnerable flesh. He converts his flesh into instrument alone.

There is, of course, a further meaning to flesh for man. In addition to being an instrument for the mastery of the world and a site for the disclosure of the world to man, it is also the form under which man reveals himself to others. This is what the existentialists meant when they observed that man not only *has* a body, he *is* body. Man reveals himself to others under the form of flesh. Again, therefore, insofar as a man ruthlessly instrumentalizes his flesh for the sake of the mastery of the world, he withdraws not only from the uncontrollable creation that im-

pinges upon his flesh but also from his fellows, who know him
as he is only in and through the full impact of his flesh. It is not
an accident that the culture which celebrates man's triumph over
nature, as though this triumph alone were his destiny, is also
obsessed in its literature with the theme of sexual impotence.
Man is created to be lord of the garden, but not alone. Lordship
alone means loneliness for man. Thus he is placed not only *over*
the creation but *with* his fellow man. Insofar as avarice reduces a
man's life to ownership and control, it produces certain further
sins against the neighbor.

Covetousness and the neighbor

Covetousness can cause sins both of commission and omission
against the neighbor. Usually we think of the former. The common tradition lists treachery, fraud, falsehood, perjury, and violence among the daughters of covetousness. But the sins of omission are no less serious, even though they may be less spectacular.
Absorbed in the frantic pursuit of possessions, the avaricious man
becomes oblivious to his neighbor's need. His sin produces a
serious isolation from his neighbor. Appropriately, the miser always appears in fiction as a withdrawn personality, suspicious in
his relations to man and God. Such a man may not have to appear in the law courts and be judged guilty of a crime, but surely
he stands so judged in Scripture. Strikingly enough, the "goats" in
Matthew 25 are not thieves and frauds, perjurers and murderers.
They are guilty simply of the sins of neglect. They fail to give a
cup of water to the thirsty, clothing to the naked, and comfort to
those in prison. Medieval man had a fine term for summarizing
all those sins of omission that result from avarice: insensibility to
mercy.

Such avarice is not simply a personal sin. Corporations, as well
as misers, can be ruthlessly inhuman in the acquisition of goods.
Ironically, men who would be quick to criticize the miser for his
inhumanity toward his fellow man will nevertheless defend to
the hilt the very same sin, when committed in the name of cor-

poration profits. Sharp dealings with competitors and woeful neglect of the towns and cities in which companies are located are no less sins because they are committed under the shelter of a corporate name. Only recently, observers have pointed out that racial strife in certain of our cities might have been materially reduced if certain corporations and unions had accepted their responsibilities as institutions of major influence in their region. Ironically, while proud of their economic prowess, they have acted as though they were moral, civic, and social nonentities. There is a certain truth, of course, to the observation that institutions must distinguish between their primary tasks and their secondary responsibilities. But it is equally true that these secondary responsibilities can be the test of the probity with which those primary tasks are discharged. The good example of certain corporations and unions on civic and social issues is evidence that occluded behavior is not inherent in the profit system, at least not so inherent as to furnish a morally convincing excuse to the avaricious.

A further order of offense against the neighbor that covetousness may produce occurs when a man makes the neighbor himself the object of his avarice. In this case, one's fellow man, rather than external goods, becomes the object of possession and control. In earlier cultures, this sin, at its extreme limit, was slavery. Certain persons—subjects, wives, children, workers, or servants—were treated as though they were owned outright, subject to absolute lordship. In contemporary culture, this sin takes a less obvious but potentially no less degrading form. The pleasures of ownership have been replaced by the pleasures of manipulation. Now it is the voter, the consumer, the worker, who is reduced to an object of the techniques of management and control. Revolutionary literature once abounded with protest against the reduction of the neighbor to a chattel; and modern existentialist literature abounds in protest against the reduction of the neighbor to an object manipulated and controlled. In both cases, instead of hearing one's neighbor, one handles him. This takes place in the slave market, to be sure, but also at the modern advertising conference and the cocktail party.

Just as the question had to be raised as to whether all ownership and control of external goods is sinful, so the question must
be posed with respect to possessing the neighbor—except in this
case, even more discriminately. A distinction must be made between ownership and control.

Ruled out altogether for the Christian is the ownership of
of another human being. Man is placed over the garden, but
with his neighbor. This placement rules out ownership, whether
overt or covert, and whether directed toward a slave, a child, or a
dependent friend. No rite is more pertinent on this subject than
the sacrament of baptism. The apostle Paul interpreted the sacrament in the context of the deliverance of the Israelites from
their slavery in Egypt to the promised land. Correspondingly,
Christ's deliverance of man from the slavery of sin carries with it
the establishment of the free man before God. Seen in this light,
the sacrament has revolutionary consequences for the human institution of slavery. Would-be slaveowners, managers, parents,
and authoritarian personalities, are dispossessed of their possessions. Appropriately enough, the sacrament of infant baptism
symbolically represents this fact. Parents must take their own
children—those in life whom they are most tempted to assume
that they own—and surrender them into the hands of God.

But if the outright ownership of other human beings is ruled
out, what of limited modes of control? Does not the organization
of man's political, economic, cultural, and even domestic life
inevitably involve certain relations of super- and sub-ordination
between human beings? Is it proper to judge these relationships
sinful, or if not sinful (because inevitable), is it proper to judge
them unfortunate? ". . . This is the exalted melancholy of our
fate, that every *Thou* in our world must become an *It*."*

Clearly, by way of first principle: the absolute control of
one person by another is unjustifiable. Augustine observes that
the placement of man *over* man can have at best a *relative* justification. The control of children by parent, students by teachers,

* Martin Buber, *I and Thou* (2d ed.; New York: Charles Scribner's Sons,
1958), p. 16. The italics are found in the text.

employees by employers, has its final justification and therefore its rigorous limit only insofar as this relation of control serves and enlarges ways in which men can be *with* one another. It is a theological error to elevate these relations of super- and sub-ordination into a law of nature, as though they were themselves proper ends for man. A fatal element of pomposity obtrudes itself into human existence whenever being *over* another person becomes an end in itself. The Lord himself undercut such pomposity when he accepted the disturbing forms of a servant, a waiter, and a footwasher among men.

Once limited in this fashion, however, a certain positive place must be given to ordered human community even when it involves, admittedly, elements of control and, consequently, certain elements of indirection and incompleteness in contacts between human beings. Not all human relations can be lived out at the level of a direct, immediate, "I-Thou" encounter, and the fact that they cannot need not be bemoaned. Teachers, leaders, doctors, and especially fathers must often accept without false dismay the incompleteness of their contacts with those over whom they exercise authority. In doing their limited jobs, they may well serve a person whose fellowship they never directly enjoy. Indeed, if they exceed these limits, they may succeed only in making the relationship forced and superficial. At the same time, students, subjects, patients, and especially sons must often accept without resentment the limited character of their contact with those responsible for them. And they may well be grateful for such limitations, rather than have imposed upon them the banalities of a father who is only a pal or the dangers of a demagogue who pretends to immediate identity with the will of the people. Only a false, devouring, religious romanticism strains for an "immediacy" or a "breakthrough" in every human encounter at the expense of institutional discipline and restraint.

Only a false messianism fears that the neighbor's integrity as a person is damaged irreparably by a failure to break through to such immediacy. The neighbor is a subject, already, as posited by God. My limited, or bad, handling of him can neither establish nor deny the neighbor as a person. When I fear that my handling of my neighbor can have these consequences, when I fear that my neighbor dies as a subject when I treat him as an object, then I have retreated to the last secret refuge of covetousness toward the neighbor, not by actually seeking to possess him but by audaciously assuming that I can.

Covetousness and the self

The man who sins against his neighbor by seeking to reduce him to an object suffers a modulation in his own being. He begins to understand himself as a commodity, subject to manipulation and control. He reckons with certain capital sums at his disposal. His intelligence, personality, and appearance, his education and contacts, become assets—and liabilities—over which he presides with satisfaction and anxiety. Whenever a man ceases to open out toward other human beings in their freedom as subjects, he no longer relates to himself as a free subject. He seeks to reduce himself to an object (even though privileged among objects) within his own grasp and control.

Existentialist literature has been especially sensitive to this third dimension of the sin. In the language of Martin Buber, the "I" in the authentic relationship of an "I" to a "Thou" is not the same "I" as in the inauthentic relationship of an "I" to an "it." When a man reduces the world to a field of objects, he debases not only the world but himself.

Gabriel Marcel does not mention the word avarice, but, in effect, the French Catholic philosopher turns it into the most comprehensive of sins. Marcel distinguishes between two fundamental orders: the authentic order of being and the inauthentic order of having. Avarice thereby becomes the most fundamental way in which man defects from his essential being as man. The essence of human existence is openness to God and to one's neighbor. Man renounces his authentic being for the inauthentic realm of having whenever he reduces his neighbor and himself to objects at his disposal. This renunciation, moreover, is not simply the peculiar sin of the "practical man," who converts all objects in the world, including himself, into possessable and controllable entities. It has been prepared for in principle by the self-interpretations of "theoretical man," insofar as the Western philosophical tradition has usually interpreted man as an isolable substance, defined by certain *properties* (reason, will, and appetite) which this substance *possesses*. Philosophers as well as practical men, therefore, have operated at the inauthentic level of having.

Martin Heidegger has characterized this reduction of man to a disposable object in terms still closer to the language of avarice. He uses specifically the terms: *Vorhandene* and *Zuhandene*. The *Vorhandene* refers to objects within the world as they are viewed by theoretical man—literally, objects "before one's hand." The *Zuhandene* refers to objects within the world as they appear for use by practical man—literally, objects "at hand." Heidegger argues that man profanes himself whenever he understands himself in the reflected light of his view and use of objects within the world which are at his disposal.

It is no accident that Heidegger relies explicitly on the metaphor of the hands to describe the inauthentic self. Existentialism, at large, whether in its theist or atheist versions, has been driven by a powerful sense of the distinction between the sacred and the profane, the authentic and inauthentic; and avarice, as we have suggested, is the peculiar sin of the secular or profane man. In its enmity to the profane, existentialism has been the relentless enemy of avarice.

Some of the existentialists, however, must be rejected on the subject of avarice because of their tendency to exaggerate. First, they have so extended the scope of the sin as to include all of man's having under the shadow of the fall. They overlook the decisive fact that having is not in itself sinful, the hands are not in themselves profane, the secular order is not in itself inauthentic. Second, they have so extended the scope of avarice as to reduce all other sins to this one alone. Sin may be religious as well as secular in character. Avarice is peculiar to the secular man. Impurity of heart, faintheartedness, envy, hatred, and lust are often, although not inevitably, the sins peculiar to the religious man. They often give evidence that man is controlled rather than controller, possessed rather than possessor, of himself and his world. And yet, just as surely, they violate a man's life in God.

Covetousness and God

Each sin presents itself as tempting. The context for each sin in its temptingness is a sense of the absence of God. This is clearly the case for pride, idolatry, and faintheartedness. The serpent talks things over with Eve while God is not there. The Israelites follow Aaron's lead in the worship of the golden calf while God is somewhere on the mountaintop. The Israelites recoil from entrance into the promised land because the strength of the Amorites is so visible, while the power of God seems so lacking. The denial of God, in all three cases, would seem to reflect an actual state of affairs (God's absence) rather than to defy God's presence. The situation is the same for the avaricious man. The hands of God seem so remote and his own hands so near. Why not rely on them as the effective source of safety and salvation? Who can say that God actually holds men in his hands? Is it not safer to take responsibility into one's own hand from an absentee, far-distant, nonexistent God?

But this does not mean that the man of avarice automatically does without the notion of a god. Divinity may have a place in the religious systems of avarice in one of two forms. If I am poor and want something, then God may have a place as the object of my petitions. If I am rich and have everything, then God may have a place as the object of my gratitude. The first is poor man's religion, the religion of petition; it is directed to the future action of God. The second is rich man's religion, the religion of gratitude; it is directed to the past action of God. In the first case, avarice, discovering the uncertainty of its control, has recourse to God as prop. In the second case, avarice, wanting to establish the sanctity of its control, has recourse to God as its dead patron. Religion, in each case, develops in the following way.

Insofar as I seek to draw creaturely goods into the circle of my ownership and control, they betray a certain intransigence. They refuse to yield entirely to my efforts at domination. I want money, but I don't get enough. I manage my children, but I am not able to dominate them wholly in accordance with my notions of their own best interests. An absolute control over creaturely possessions eludes me. I discover, in effect, my poverty. Therefore I have recourse to God as a prop—one whom I petition to give me more possessions or to insure the ones I have. He becomes a kind of cosmic extension of my own hands. In his handiness he helps me to extend the sphere over which I exercise control. This is the special function of a god who has become the prop of a human community whether an ecclesiastical hierarchy, a political party, a national culture, or a racial minority or majority. God becomes the possession who gives cohesion and coherence to all other possessions. He may be relied upon to bless friends and curse enemies, console losses and support gains; he promises help in all future adventures in avarice, and men can invoke his name to protect them whenever a cold wind blows that threatens to dispossess them of everything.

Not that petition for God's help has no place in the Christian life. There is Christian petition for rain, shelter, daily bread, companionship, and good health. These apply to the needs of man. But if I address my petitions to a god who is no more than a prop, then I am most eager, once he has given me service, to have him on his way. I desire his company no more than I would want a bellhop to linger in the room once he has brought me my tray and ice. In effect, I want an absentee lord, one who is handy but not my companion. And herein lies my despair. I am like a hotel-room solitary who calls for everything but what he needs most.

The religion of gratitude develops in a somewhat different way. Since I am rich, I do not need a god to give me more than I have, but I do have one need that I am not able to meet by myself. I need some way of demonstrating to the world, and to myself, that my position as possessor is in good order. Therefore I need a god who has given me what I have and to whom I can

render thanks without undue discomfort to my position. I need a
dead patron.

This is the religious system that has been popular among the
wealthier nations and classes of the West. It has affected Christian preaching to this day and it has influenced those very sermons that would seem most directed against the sin of avarice:
the stewardship sermons of the middle-class Protestant church.

Christian preaching directed against avarice has usually relied
on the concept of stewardship. By definition, a steward is an
official in charge of the domestic affairs of a household, accountable for his behavior to the master of the house. According to
Scripture, men are stewards of the Lord, and derive from him all
that they own and control, and consequently owe him an ac-
counting for their use of those goods and powers with which they
have been entrusted. The notion of stewardship, so understood,
both establishes and limits a man's use of his possessions.

As it is often preached, however, the force of the theme of
stewardship is weakened because it is expounded in the context
of a doctrine of God wholly friendly to the interests of the avaricious man. Historically, the notion of God especially congenial to
the emergence of a secular civilization is that of deism.

The deist affirms that there is a god—a supreme being—who
created the world and its inhabitants, but that his work of creation took place in the distant past. He is the creator to whom
everything can be traced back, as it were, to its first cause. But he
is not alive today and tomorrow. His work finished, he has withdrawn conveniently to the background, while man occupies the
foreground, owning and mastering his world through his own
vital powers. Such a god is wholly friendly to the emergence of
secular man, and certainly to the secular man in his sin, in that
he becomes the absentee Lord. Absent himself, he allows man to
center his life in his own possessions and control. The deist god is
untroublesome. It is possible to forget him. He barely exists. He
intervenes feebly, only once or twice a year, when stewardship
sermons gently remind us that all our talents and fortunes are
ultimately derived from him.

Covetousness and the Word of God

Jesus does not preach in terms so convenient for avarice.
God the Father did not create the world in the distant past and
then withdraw from the scene. He surprises men with his presence today and tomorrow. He throws off balance the calculations
of the avaricious man. If avarice is the sin in which man reduces
everything to human calculation and control, it is revealing that
Jesus chose an event which is wholly amazing, incalculable, and
crushing as parable for God's encounter with the sinner. That
event is death.

> "Take heed, and beware of all covetousness; for a man's life
> does not consist in the abundance of his possessions." And he
> told them a parable, saying, "The land of a rich man brought
> forth plentifully; and he thought to himself, 'What shall I do,
> for I have nowhere to store my crops?' And he said, 'I will do
> this: I will pull down my barns, and build larger ones; and
> there I will store all my grain and my goods. And I will say
> to my soul, 'Soul, you have ample goods laid up for many
> years; take your ease, eat, drink, be merry.' But God said to
> him, 'Fool! This night your soul is required of you; and the
> things you have prepared, whose will they be?' "
>
> Luke 12:15–20

The event of death—its suddenness, its unexpectedness, and its
finality—upsets the calculations of the avaricious man. The point
is the same in the parable of the unfaithful steward (Luke
12:41–48), who relies on his master's absence to do as he pleases
only to be surprised by his unexpected homecoming.

The parables of Jesus exclude a pallid deism as a doctrinal
basis for Christian preaching on the subject of avarice. For death
always reaches man as startling news that intersects and inter-
rupts his ongoing world. The deist god is no longer newsworthy.
Beyond his early work, there is nothing further to say, nothing to
proclaim about his deeds among men. The real difference between deism and Christian theism is not that the deists affirm a

God who is creator alone, while the Christians go on, additionally, to affirm a God who is redeemer and sanctifier of men. Rather, these two further additions are such as to revise the meaning of all three activities on the part of God. God's work as creator, re-creator, and glorifier of men always reaches man as a newsworthy event. It can never become a doctrinal *basis* for his life, as though God were somehow underfoot, while man builds his barns, harvests his fields, and collects his treasures above. The view of God as *terra firma,* the silent background to human life, was broken up for the Christian church when God, surprisingly, unexpectedly, and irrevocably, broke open the tomb in which Jesus was buried and raised him from the dead. This event was critical in the history of human avarice. For in a sense the success of human avarice—the whole attempt to keep the world under lock and key—depends upon keeping God under lock and key. Thus it was that Pilate said to them, " 'You have a guard of soldiers; go, make it as secure as you can.' So they went and made the sepulchre secure by sealing the stone and setting a guard" (Matthew 27:65–66). In breaking through this lock and guard, God refused to be the God that men, in their avarice, would want him to be, the God removed from sight, the absentee Lord, the dead patron.

This refusal on God's part to be the dead patron that the avaricious want him to be means that they themselves are heading for a death. For this reason as well, Jesus appeals to the event of death in his parable. The possessor must be dispossessed. He who thinks he has everything has nothing. He who would like to be a lord, holding everything he needs in his hands, must be held by the Lord who died holding nothing in his hands. The possessor must be dispossessed and repossessed by this Lord.

The only difficulty with accepting this further implication of the parable of death is that it ignores the rest of Jesus' teaching on the subject of avarice. There is also the episode of the rich young man whom Jesus commands to sell all that he has and give it to the poor if he would inherit eternal life (Matthew 19:16–22). Here the teaching of Jesus is not simply the negative command to give up but the positive command to give out to the neighbor. The true opposite of the tight-fistedness of avarice is not the empty-handedness of death, but the open-handedness of love. This open-handedness is the characteristic of the divine life itself, as the Father gives all things to the Son, and as the Son, in turn, does not grasp at equality with God but gives himself to men, accepting even death, to bring them to eternal life. God has dealt open-handedly with men and summons them to deal open-handedly with one another. This is the final, and equally radical, instruction of Jesus concerning covetousness. His instruction is sealed in his own self-giving death and confirmed by God in his resurrection from the dead. This is the disturbing and gracious Lord who rules.

No sooner said, however, than the questions begin: Was the Lord indeed raised from the dead? Is the Lord truly alive, or did his disciples merely steal away his corpse? Does he rule even now, or did he vanish forever under the rule of death? Will he come once again, or has the church only projected its own unverifiable wishes across the heavens? These are the questions of avarice in its temptingness. God is absent, his hands remote, and his return unlikely; let me then build my barns, harvest my crops, beat my servants, and get a little drunk. Here is my salvation, in the use and abuse of what lies near at hand.

The force of these questions and their tempting solution in avarice is enough to prompt the Lord's own question:

When the Son of man comes, will he find faith?

The Sins of
Man with His Neighbor

4 The Sin Against the Brother:
ENVY

Gregory the Great placed envy among the seven capital sins. It came immediately after pride, followed by anger, dejection, avarice, gluttony, and lust. In this book, envy follows avarice because both have to do with possessions; for this reason, they are often confused. The distinction between them lies partly in the fact that envy, in each and every case, has to do with the socially disruptive impact of possessions. But avarice can also be socially disruptive. What, then, distinguishes envy from avarice?

The classical tradition had a fine way of maintaining a distinction between the two. The covetous man wants to possess the good of his neighbor, whereas the envious man, first and foremost, regrets it. He grieves over his neighbor's good luck. That is why John of Damascus called envy a species of sorrow and defined it specifically as "sorrow for another's good."

La Rochefoucauld explored the nasty underside of this definition when he observed, "Few are able to suppress in themselves a secret satisfaction at the misfortunes of their friends." If envy is sorrow for the neighbor's good, then it can also produce a certain exquisite delight in his downfall.

Envy enjoys a specific natural habitat. It finds itself most at

home, as Aristotle observed, in relations between equals; it nour-
ishes itself on struggles between competitors. Let Pablo Casals be
praised for a stunning performance and I am not likely to feel
envy, for I am neither a nonagenarian nor a cellist. However, let
someone publish an excellent essay on envy while I am writing
this chapter (as, indeed, Angus Wilson has done), and I am likely
to know the subtle pressures of this sin.

In the Bible, envy breaks out between competitors or, more
specifically, between those most intense of competitors: brothers.
It appears in the relations between Cain and Abel, Jacob and
Esau, Joseph and his brothers, the elder brother and the prodigal
son—all of them squabbling over a parental blessing. The classical scriptural portrait of envy, however, is none of these but
rather the story of King Saul. For it was Saul who heard the
women singing one day:

> "Saul has slain his thousands, and David his ten thousands."
> And Saul was very angry, and this saying displeased him; he
> said, "They have ascribed to David ten thousands, and to me
> they have ascribed thousands; and what more can he have
> but the kingdom?" And Saul eyed David from that day on.
>
> I Samuel 18:7–9

It is revealing that I Samuel uses the pharse "and Saul *eyed*
David," for the Latin word from which our own word "envy"
derives is *invidia*. It means literally "to look upon," and eventually came to mean "to look maliciously upon." Envy, above all
else, is a sin of the eyes—the eyes riveted on others with malice.
Thomas Aquinas quite properly counts it among the vices contrary to charity.

Envy might be classified among the sins of the religious man.
Saul "eyes" David. He pays him heed. Around other men Saul
can afford to be relaxed. But with David he must always be on
the alert—attentive and observant. He is in the presence of
someone who seems to have all the luck, the boon, the *mana* from
heaven, that he himself lacks.

Our rockets have flown their thousands

It has been a favorite pastime among moralists to assign particular sins to particular social groups. More than one Protestant preacher in the Victorian era betrayed his bourgeois sympathies by charging the working class with the special vice of envy! Recently Angus Wilson has indicted resentful Europeans of the same sin vis-à-vis the Americans and the Russians.

Obviously there is a danger in delivering a moral broadside against an entire class or nation. Nevertheless there is a meaningful sense in which an entire people, class, or nation can be religiously obsessed in the fashion of Saul. It even has a special application today to the national self-understanding of Americans. Specifically, for the first time in our national history, Americans are in a position to understand the predicament of Saul.

As a country we are no longer in the position of David among the nations. At one time we were the nation in obvious ascendancy—the land the gods had blessed, a people who fought their battles with confidence and who displayed the easygoing generosity that the Davids of the earth can afford.

But now our weapons are threatened by the rocketry of another. A new David, a strange incalculable figure, has appeared on the horizon. For the first time we have been forced to watch apprehensively the movements of another, just as Saul once made up his mind to "eye David from that day on."

Our rockets have flown their thousands. And the Russians' their ten thousands. And what more can they have but the earth? How tempting to take a javelin while this David plays his harp, and to smite him against the wall with it! So far, the policies of our government have not been determined by men subject to the malady of Saul. But, since Sputnik, no one can deny the pressure of this emotion in our national life.

Of equal importance with the peculiar crisis in our national self-understanding, however, is the more personal and intimate way in which men find themselves in Saul's predicament. We live in a society that perhaps as much as any other has refined its social life in such a way as to pit equals against one another. Americans segregate themselves instinctively into their respective age groups and economic levels—pre-teens with pre-teens, teen-agers with teen-agers, young marrieds with young marrieds, the middle-aged with their peers in affluent neighborhoods, and old-sters in St. Petersburg.

In one college recently about one-half of the members of the freshman class had been valedictorians, salutatorians, or class presidents in the high schools from which they came. Put that many young Davids together and you are bound to get some Sauls. Immense pressures build up today in the highly competi-tive atmosphere of school, college, corporation, and neighbor-hood that tend to make envy almost a natural coefficient of life.

Today no matter how solid a man's success may be—or at least no matter how solid it may appear to his neighbor—in some relation in life he knows what it feels like to be Saul. He knows what it feels like to be on the short end of a blessing, galled by the very sight of the man who has the luck.

The mark of envy

In *The Seven Deadly Sins** Angus Wilson has made a very shrewd comment about the distinguishing feature of envy. Every other capital sin, he observes, offers a certain measure of satisfac-tion in its early stages, even though its ultimate consequence is morbid self-destruction. Envy alone, however, is peculiarly with-out gratification at every stage. At every point, "Envy is impo-tent, numbed with fear, yet never ceasing in its appetite; and it knows no gratification save endless self-torment."

Envy has another distinguishing mark, however, that should not go unnoticed. It is the one sin that a man rarely, if ever, confesses. He does not mind admitting that he is proud or de-jected or, even, lustful. But that he envies another, if he *really* envies, he rarely admits.

* Angus Wilson *et al., The Seven Deadly Sins* (New York: William Morrow & Co., 1962).

Of course, on occasion we say: "Oh, how wonderful! I envy you." This is the sort of phrase we use when we don't really envy, when perhaps out of kindness we want to encourage a friend who is down in the dumps. When we really envy another, then we keep our mouths shut. We never speak about it. At best, it shows up indirectly. As the saying goes, we turn green with envy.

Yet when envy really takes hold of a man's life, it can secretly govern much of what he does: it can be the unaccountable source of dejection; it can flood a man's body with lust and avarice; and it can moisten a man's tongue with malice. For when envy attains ruling power over a man, it blurts out by producing several of the other sins mentioned by Gregory the Great: avarice, dejection, and malice.

Envy and malice

The envious man has a peculiar gift for chipping away at the reputation of others: praising them with one phrase, damning them subtly with another. He applies the severest standards of justice to others, usually finding them lucky beyond their deserts—in wealth, looks, health, and other tokens of the good life. He is especially adept—almost an expert—at noticing the defects of others: their stupidity, talkativeness, or conceit.

Admittedly, some people are stupid and others are talkative and vain; virtue does not require one to be blind to these facts. But what is it that makes a man take the fault of another and make of it his obsession? When he is sick with envy, he can do this.

When a man sees the head of another garlanded with blessings, his hands graced with the power of God, then he hates and seeks to cancel the other out. Cain murders; Esau rages helplessly; Joseph's brothers throw him into a pit; the elder brother of the prodigal grumbles to his father; and Saul takes his javelin and hurls it at David. The envious man in every age finds his own peculiar weapons, his verbal darts and poisoned barbs, and seeks to penetrate and destroy the honor of another.

It would be wrong to strain for a comparison between ordinary life and the classical biblical passage at points where there is none. Usually men do not understand themselves to be in a situation quite so hopeless as that of Saul, where the division between the successful and the defeated is so sharp. Usually the situation is more ambiguous. Each person finds himself jockeying in a whole field of competitors for blessings, where the ins and the outs, the haves and the have-nots, and the blessings themselves shift and change each day. Saul, however, grieved over David's possession of the supreme blessing of them all, the power of God, from which he himself was removed.

The extremity of the story does not free men from its force. It does not exempt men from the need to be reminded that envy produces malice.

Hypocrisy, dejection, and avarice

Because envy is a sin among brothers, it strikes precisely in those intimate relations where love is supposed to rule. Thus, envy produces hypocrisy. When a man hears of the good fortune of a friend, he can say one thing but feel another. He speaks of his delight, but sometimes he has to apply a certain mechanical force to draw this delight up from an inner reserve. Saul gives David his own daughter for a wife. But he is careful to send David into battle where hopefully the Philistines will slaughter him. At the same time that a man declares his friendship for another, he can rejoice in seeing him cut down to size.

If envy is sorrow for the neighbor's good, it can also produce a sorrow over one's own lack of good. Envy produces dejection.

How depressing it can be to witness the blessing of another. How dejecting to struggle among the have-nots. A girl is depressed by the beauty of her sister. A man grits his teeth when another is promoted in his corporation. Mediocre students find another's display of brilliance depressing.

The successful belong to the major leagues—the league of gods —with the top jobs, the right clubs, youth, money, property, the right beau, husband or wife; while the dejected belong to a minor league—a bush league of overnight buses, bad meals, and miserable batting averages.

Deep dejection of this sort suggests that envy may produce not only a malice directed against others but also a malice directed toward one's self. A man may not wish simply to cancel another man out, but, by implication, to cancel himself out. This is what lies behind the sigh: "I wish I were in his shoes." A person denies the spot where he is, the gifts that have been given him. He wants to occupy the place of another. His envy produces dejection and self-hatred, at the root of which is ingratitude.

Perhaps this explains the ironical treatment of envy at the hands of the artist. Envy is a sin of the eyes, and yet artists have portrayed her as blind. Giotto shows envy as a figure with the tongue of a serpent that strikes against her own eyes. Dante describes the envious as those whose eyes are sewn shut. Perhaps the specific blindness of envy is ingratitude. Grief for the good of another is blindness to the self's own treasure from God.

Although envy and avarice are distinguishable, one sin may give rise to the other. Specifically, envy can set loose desires. It is as simple as two children playing on the floor. Both ignore a toy. But let one of them touch it, and it then becomes infinitely precious to them both.

While this may be amusing or irritating in children, it is much less dignified in a whole civilization. Worthless items are produced, and desires for them kindled by envy. Every modern advertising man knows that envy whips up the fires of avarice; indeed, our advertising and industrial systems rely on it.

The religious life of the envious

It was pointed out earlier that the sin of avarice produces two forms of religion: the poor man's religion of petition and the rich man's religion of gratitude. The latter is totally absent from the man of envy. He has nothing to be grateful about. He feels his poverty with every crust of bread he eats. In some cases, no possession whatsoever could cure him of his despondency. He secretly disparages himself. Were something to become his, it would lose its value immediately. He would have to hunt for something else in the possession of his neighbor from which to take his bearings. He would not feel at home in the world again until he was yearning for someone else's riches. A feeling of poverty belongs to his equilibrium in sin.

In other cases, the envious man has an exalted notion of himself. But once again he is incapable of gratitude. Self-inflated, he finds life unbearable because it fails to render him his just due. He feels lacking in metaphysical acclaim. Indeed, no possession would be enough to close the gap between his sense of his just deserts and the tokens of life that actually come his way. There is one thing alone that would satisfy him and that is the dark satisfaction of seeing his undeserving neighbor dispossessed. This alone would give him the feeling that the universe was on his side. Short of this occurrence (and even with it) he remains a poor man, incapable of gratitude.

Envy can lead only to the poor man's religion of petition. It feeds on an emptiness. The petitions of the envious are poisonous compared with those of the avaricious. There is something positive—almost wholesome—about the requests of the avaricious man. After all, he seeks only the good things he lacks. He appeals to God—as to a handyman—to give him what he wants. The envious man, however, wants God to act as a henchman to deprive another. He offers a kind of intercessory prayer in reverse. His silent petitions make appeal to God for the destruction of another: O Lord, lower his profits for next year. Dry up his chrysanthemum beds. Blight his roses. Bless him with boll weevils. Let him be caught in his treachery by the boss.

When the envious man takes to invoking the powers that be to do their worst, it is not too long before he gives them a little assistance. In this case, envy has fulfilled itself in betrayal. "Out of envy, he delivered him up."

The Christian solution to the problem of envy cannot take the form of moralizing on the subject. This was the customary solution of those preachers who converted I Samuel into a morality tale. They contrasted good King David with tragic King Saul, and they exhorted men to mimic the magnanimity of David and avoid Saul's small-mindedness. The difficulty with this solution is that a show of magnanimity is itself just one more possession in the treasury of the rich that exacerbates envy. How much more obnoxious David must have been, precisely because he was magnanimous! Liberality of outlook is precisely what the envious in their poverty cannot achieve.

A moralistic interpretation of the incident from I Samuel overlooks two important complications in the story. First, it ignores David's own tragic decline into the position of Saul. David himself ends up in an impoverished position, a middle-aged adulterer with civil war on his hands. Second, it ignores the still-later event in which this whole episode has its resolution. The Christian church has always interpreted the story in the light of the career of Jesus Christ, "Great David's greater Son." The narrative does not break off with the rise of young David and the hapless decline of Saul any more than an earlier narrative breaks off with the rise of Joseph as the Pharaoh's right-hand man and the starvation of his father and brothers. The important point in the latter is that God eventually fed, through Joseph, both Joseph and his brothers. So also the blessing in David points toward the future. It beckons specifically toward a son of David, one who will feed both rising young men and aging kings in their decline. This is the context in which Christians have always read this story, a context that makes it much more than a little episode in the long history of the quarrel between the haves and the have-nots. The Gospel of Matthew begins very simply: "The book of the genealogy of Jesus Christ, the son of David. . . ." (Matthew 1:1) The church service confirms this context: "Hail to the Lord's Anointed/Great David's greater Son."

Jesus Christ breaks the power of the sin not so much because he demonstrates a virtuous life, free of envying, but because he comes to the envious themselves. He comes not only to the Davids of the world but also to the Sauls. If this claim is more than rhetoric, it requires a final statement about Saul.

At the hidden center of Saul's experience of envy is a double sense of poverty: first, his loss of fighting prowess, and second, his sense of abandonment at the hands of God. This second experience of impoverishment is more important than the first. If Saul had not felt the presence of God in and through his fighting strength, he would not have mourned its loss so inconsolably. It would be possible to survive the one loss if it were not tied up with the other. "Saul was afraid of David, because the Lord was with him but had departed from Saul." The passage makes it clear, moreover, that Saul's problem is not simply his own impoverishment but, even more cruelly, David's enrichment. If Saul's strength had only drained away quietly into the ground, or if the Lord had retreated to parts unknown, then things might have been better. But unfortunately, Saul's loss is David's gain. Indeed, Saul is poor *because* David is richer. "Saul has slain his thousands, and David his ten thousands."

There is no redemption for Saul, then, unless God comes to him and stands with him, where Saul himself stands, subject to the anguish of abandonment, and to the indignities of another's possession of power. But this is precisely where the son of God stands when he cries, "My God, my God, why hast thou forsaken me?" He is executed by those who possess full moral and political power. Righteous possessors of the law of God judge him as unrighteous, and powerful executors of the law of the state do away with him in his powerlessness. Nevertheless he stands there in the position of Saul and cries, "Father, into thy hands I commit my spirit." In this act and with this cry, the King of the Jews stands fast with fallen kings, judging them with his obedience, forgiving them with his presence, and relieving them of every need for sorrow. It is a sense of God's absence on which envy thrives; it is the experience of God's absence that God the Son has faithfully borne.

Once the man of envy discovers that God stands with him in his poverty, he makes a further discovery. If he looks sideways at the rich man whom he envied, he sees that God has unexpectedly answered his prayers. He discovers not a rich man at all but someone acutely in need like himself. In the presence of Jesus, David is also poor—as poor as Saul—and not just because the innocent young shepherd, with a shining career ahead of him, has declined into a middle-aged adulterer with rebellion on his hands. David is needy from beginning to end. He is also needy before the self-expending love of his own son.

For the career of David, like all careers built on a possession, finds itself raging against a Lord who comes into possession of the world by dispossessing himself. Jesus enters upon his ministry clothed with the titles of messianic office. People recognize him as the possessor of messianic power. He is the son of David, inheritor of a king's office; he is a prophet and teacher, possessor of the tradition of the law; he is physician and priest, dispenser of sacral power to the sick and the sinful. But he dies on a cross, wholly dispossessed—a king with no subjects, a teacher with no pupils, a healer who bleeds, a priest with no sacrifice to make other than himself. If he is indeed the son of God, the Lord of the earth, the Messiah who will be all in all, then what man stands wealthy before him? Where is the power in money, virtue, high office, good looks, or good luck before his own self-expending love?

Before Jesus, all are poor without exception, but also, all are rich without exception. For although men are divested of everything, they are not left with nothing; they are cherished by the very love that divests them. This is the peculiar blessing in which the whole scriptural record of blessing comes to rest. God has set down in the midst of the envious a wealth, a blessing, a glory far more substantial than all the glories for which they struggle, backbite, and grow cold toward one another. Even while men busy themselves in the works of envy, snatching after one glory or another, the son of the most high did not envy the glory of the Father but emptied himself to let men receive his blessing without envy and malice.

This blessing is distinct from all others in that it does not give to a man a possession that separates him from his neighbor. He is rich in God but without possessions. By every other blessing, a man is separated from his fellow man. One man's joy is another man's deprivation. One teacher receives tenure on a faculty; another does not. One man's robust health mocks the illness of a friend. But to possess the love of God in this Jew, whose tenure as a teacher was three short years, and whose body was exhausted on a cross, is to receive a blessing which at long last does not divide men into the haves and the have-nots, the brilliant and the stupid, the beautiful and the homely, the busy and the lonely, the Jew and the Greek, the slave and the free. In Christ, "there is no distinction. . . ." (Romans 3:22) Before him, all men—without exception—know total poverty and total wealth.

The fulfillment of the history of blessing in Jesus Christ is the basis for the Apostle's summons to walk honestly together without envying. This summons, however, may come differently to those who are spoiled by riches and to those who are poor in earthly goods. To the rich it may mean, first and foremost: Put aside all the little blessings and good-luck charms and carefully cultivated assets that have been treated as everything. Why dwell on another man's house, when both have a dwelling in the household of God? Why be obsessed with the undeserved "good luck" of a neighbor, when no one has deserved forgiveness at the hands of God? Why should one gently compete with friends to appear to suffer the most, when God carries him and his competitor, shouldering the real burdens of the world on their behalf?

But to the poor the Christian message about envy does not enjoin "contentment" with one's earthly possessions, and yet it is also directed to those who are without adequate housing, clothing, and food. It does not, however, urge on the poor a quietism that they can ill afford. The Christian message on envy is not a hypocritical message designed by the rich at the expense of the poor.

The implications for the poor man of the Christian message on the subject of envy are revolutionary. He discovers that the rich man is poor. Only when the poor man recognizes this is he truly free to act. Otherwise, he is paralyzed. He cowers in fear before the rich man, admiring his strength and collapsing upon his own impotence, or again, he dissipates his strength in sporadic outbursts of rage and envy. Martin Luther King and his followers made the discovery that the American white man was

poor, and this discovery gave impetus and discipline to a movement, the revolutionary consequences of which the white man
has yet fully to absorb. (At the same time, of course, King and
his followers have insisted that the white man is also rich—rich
in the sight of God—and this has distinguished their counsel
from the outbursts of rage by black nationalists. Among the
latter, there is an imitation of white racism that could only be
inspired by envy.)

The poverty of Christ addresses a final warning to the community of believers. The church is false whenever it behaves as
though the Lord were its own special possession. Such behavior
only inspires a certain envy or contempt in the unbeliever toward
the believer. It encourages a waspish attitude toward the WASP's.
Christ would appear to be just one more possession in the
history of the world by which men attempt to distinguish
the rich from the poor. Just as families are marked by their
possession of a common origin and memory, and nations are
distinguished by a special land, culture, and history, so the
church appears to be marked off by its special proximity to a
Savior. In this event, it would not appear that man has received
the unifying center of his life in a Lord who pulls together the
haves and the have-nots. Just one more religious movement is
added to the list of divisive possessions found in the world.

This problem for the community of believers is not solved by
the church's attempt to be more "generous" with its possession.
Too often this was the solution of the missionary movement from
the sixteenth through the nineteenth centuries. Mere generosity
with a possession shadows every gift to the unbeliever with condescension. It inspires resentment, contempt, or envy. Even
worse, it does not reflect the church's own true state of affairs.
The church has nothing to give to the unbeliever that it does not
at one and the same time have to receive with and from the
unbeliever. What preacher ever spoke a true word to his people
who did not have to hear this word with his people and, indeed,
from his people? The church before God is rich but wholly without possessions: wise in ignorance, righteous in sin, bold in

Christ but shaking inside. When the church gives, it can give faithfully only under the mark of its own neediness. Let those who experiment with envy rivet their eyes on the church in the act of its giving. There should not be much to look at.

5 The Sin Against the Enemy:
HATRED

It has been customary in the literature of the church not only to distribute the seven deadly sins according to their special locales in the human body but also to associate each sin with certain animals or fowl. Pride, for example, was rather naturally associated with the peacock, the lion, or the eagle; lechery with the goat; and gluttony with the pig. The list of associations for the capital sin closest to the vice with which we are presently concerned was much longer and, by implication, less stable. Anger was alternately depicted as a wolf, a toad, a pig, a rat, a rooster, an ass, a spider, a snake, and, at length, most appropriately, according to one theologian-zoologist, as "a figure riding on a camel, the most vicious of all animals." Not only is it arbitrary to choose a symbol from such a long list of candidates from the lower kingdoms, whose looks ought not to be held against them; this very act of symbolization tends to obscure the nature of sin. It carries the suggestion that sin is a descent from the human to the subhuman, from the rational to the emotional. In fact, it is far worse. More disconcerting than the man who reminds one of a "beast" in his treatment of other human beings is the man who is indestructibly human in the course of his inhumanity to others. Sin is not subhuman; it is frighteningly human. Those who were guilty of the most sickening of crimes in concentration camps were also, apparently, lovers of music and flowers.

The sins of man against his fellow man have to do with inhumanity rather than subhumanity. For this reason the term "hatred" is preferable to the traditional term "anger" in suggesting a perversity that takes hold in the highest reaches of the mind. The term "hatred" reflects more accurately the spiritual character of man's sin against his fellow man. Unlike anger, hatred has a way of enduring in time and organizing life around itself. It presupposes man's capacity for a certain temporal endurance of which only a spiritual being is capable. It describes a wary, spiritual mind-set that may or may not be energized by the passing force of anger.

The social context for hatred (as well as for neglect) is somewhat distinct from that of the other sins. Envy, betrayal, and lust arise in a social situation that is wholly natural to man. By nature man may be given a relationship to the brother, the friend, or the sexual partner. His sin, in each case, is his perverse response to a relation that is, in itself, innocent. In the sins of hatred and neglect, however, the relations themselves emerge, for the most part, as sin. The enemy looms as enemy in a situation that, from one side or the other or both, is already marked and riven with vice. The needy man exists as needy in a social framework marked by prior neglect. Admittedly there is a sense in which both enmity and need are the result of natural circumstances and not the expression of sin, but the Marxists and the social Darwinians exaggerated enmity, and the Malthusians and the Ricardians exaggerated poverty as natural facts of human existence. Their doctrines concerning the inevitability of class warfare, the survival of the fittest, and the permanence of poverty have often been exploited to naturalize evil and to provide moral cover for unconscionable behavior by reactionary capitalist and radical revolutionary alike. Whatever enmity and neediness may mean in nature, they cannot be allowed to obscure their primary meaning in the context of sin.

Hatred of the enemy

Who is my enemy? He is the man who, in my opinion, wishes me harm. The enemy is the man to whom I really attend, whose every move I watch. The word "religion," as we have already noted, in all probability orignally meant "alertness" and "atten-tiveness." A man's god is simply the power or powers to which he attends with his whole being. In this sense the relationship to the enemy is religious. My friends and acquaintances are people to whom I do not have to attend. From time to time I can afford to ignore them. But I cannot afford to take my eyes off my enemy. The fellow who wants my job; the country that threatens to bury my country; the race that I consider a threat to my race—these can all become my obsession. Toward his enemies, every man becomes his own Kremlinologist.

Clearly, hatred is adjacent to the sins of envy and faint-heartedness. The man of envy, like the man of hatred, gives rapt attention to his neighbor. His sin involves a certain fixing of the gaze which is religious in its intensity. Understandably, the clas-sical theologians have taken note of a spiritual connection be-tween the two sins. The man who is obsessed with the good luck of a competitor may soon be ready to inflict upon him every harm. Nevertheless, there is a difference between them. In envy, my absorption with the neighbor centers, above all else, upon his possessions. I "feel" the man I envy by way of my own lack. In hatred my feeling, if anything, is "purer." My enemy's posses-sions may feed my hatred, but they are not decisive. He does not have to be rich, I do not have to be poor; like love, hatred is not distracted by the fact of possessions.

Hatred is also akin to the sin of faintheartedness. In both attitudes, men are obsessed with their enemies. However, hatred tends to be active; fear, in itself, passive. The fainthearted recoil from their enemies in fright, whereas the malicious seek, in some way, to run out and meet their enemies, to embrace them, so to speak, by bringing down evil upon evil, even if it means, on occasion, their own destruction.

The three temporal ecstasies of hatred

Absorption with the enemy can be either retrospective—as in the case of anger—or prospective—as in the case of suspicion. The angry man looks back to the deeds that his enemy has already committed. He finds himself reviewing them over and over again. Quite naturally Osborne's play is titled *Look Back in Anger*. The very thought of past injustice causes the blood to boil. The angry man will not rest until he has done "justice" to past deeds, in all their concrete offensiveness, by finding some equally concrete mode of revenge. The medieval moralists showed some sensitivity to this problem by elevating anger, as we have seen, to one of the seven deadly sins. Thomas Aquinas observes that "the angry man desires another's evil under the aspect of just revenge."[*] The desire to punish, however, may be less a question of upholding Thomas' impersonal order of justice than a way of forcing the enemy to give as much attention to his deed as it has wrested from its victims. Only by compelling the enemy to relive his offense (or its equivalent) in all the terrible concreteness with which it has fallen upon others will the avenger find release from the terrible thrall of the event and its agent. The impotence of his rage is simply the measure of the discrepancy between the enormity of the original offense and the available modes of revenge.

No single word will describe the forward glance of hatred as aptly as anger describes its thrall with the past. Perhaps suspicion is the best term. The enemy not only outrages our sense of power because he has done something in the past; he also threatens our power because he *may* do something in the future. Thus, he puts us on our guard. We become watchful and alert to his every move. If anger looks back, suspicion runs forward. It fastens on hints and clues as to what the enemy is likely to do in the time ahead, and maintains itself in a kind of religious state of watchfulness.

Jean-Paul Sartre expanded suspicion into an entire anthropology. In his long philosophical essay, *Being and Nothingness*, he gives a fascinating account of the wary confrontation of two human beings, each trying to probe and fathom the threatening freedom of the other. Sartre explores the meaning of enmity, not only as it defines the relations of rival political powers, but also as it marks the most intimate encounters between human beings, especially the confrontation of lovers.

[*] *ST* II. ii. q 158 art. 4.

Sartre's analysis of suspicion is very much tied up with his understanding of the structure of freedom. To exist is to be free, but to be free is to be vulnerable to the intrusion into one's world of the freedom of another. Presumably I am rendered uncomfortable by this intrusion—not because the other in his freedom may do certain things harmful to me, but because his freedom itself is a disturbance to the organization of my universe. The other always meets me in his otherness, as an intruder, a stranger, an enemy, before whom I am wary. Even though I may pacify my enemy—by making treaties with him or by emphasizing "common interests," or by making love to her—underneath it all I can never rid myself of a fundamental unease. For beneath the arrangements of civilization and love, he or she remains free and, as such, an imperfection in my world. Primordial freedom means primordial enmity.

Although Sartre understands correctly a certain kind of love-less, suspicious encounter between human beings, his attempt to ground this suspicion in the very conditions of human existence is just as mistaken as the attempt of the Darwinians to ground enmity in the very conditions of biological life.* It is not because I am a man that I need to be cagey and circumspect with others, but because I am a sinful man that I am consumingly so. In sin I separate myself from my own true freedom as a freedom-for-others; consequently I sense and maintain my freedom as a freedom-against-others and I interpret the freedom of others as a freedom against me. Sartre's interpretation of human existence, in short, is wholly abstracted from the actuality and the possibility of a freedom in love. As such it is given to an excessive paranoia in its interpretation of human affairs. Nevertheless, Sartre does understand the religious dimension of suspicion, preoccupied as it is with the enemy as a future threat.

Hatred, oriented to the past, is anger; oriented to the future, suspicion; but as directed to the present, resentment. My hatred

* Some of the Darwinians understood enmity as one of the general conditions of natural life (thus warfare among men is but a specific instance of the general battle for the survival of the fittest), while Sartre understands it as one of the special conditions of human freedom.

of the enemy may focus not only on what he has done or may do, but on what he *is*. His very existence—quite apart from any specific harm he may do me in the future—provokes resentment. While the enemy lives, I cannot be myself. He upsets my notions about myself in the universe. Germany experienced this sort of enmity toward France. The very existence of France was an obstacle to the meaning of Germany. The slogan *Lebensraum* expressed Germany's frustration on this point. The very existence of the enemy withdraws the air I need. The enemy does not have to do anything. His presence in the universe is suffocating to me. I would like—I need—to see him dead.

The ideal of tolerance

There is an important spiritual ideal upon which men depend in their civilized life to combat the anger, suspicion, and resentment they direct against their enemies. Tolerance is that ideal. It usually consists of two elements: one doctrinal, the other moral.

Doctrinally, the ideal of tolerance has depended upon a belief in both the goodness and the relative uniformity of human nature. The potential goodness of all men was emphasized and the differences between them minimized. Beneath the stranger's garb there lives and breathes a man much like myself, my brother. This was the basis for tolerance in the eighteenth century. In the nineteenth and twentieth centuries this doctrine was revised to allow for fundamental differences between men, but it was helpfully accompanied either by a positive evaluation of other cultures in their variety (German idealism) or by a devaluation of one's own culture (skepticism, relativism). In either case, differences offer no obstacle to tolerance. Quite the contrary, they enrich human existence. Whatever my enemy has done, he shares with me a common humanity and he represents certain distinctive values which I should not ignore. Once I discover him in our common humanity and in his distinctive virtues, it is supposed, I will be better disposed to tolerate him.

There is an important element of truth in this line of reasoning. Hatred—despite its apparent concentration upon the enemy —is often cursed with one-sidedness and blindness. While attending to the enemy, it may fail miserably to attend to his life as it is actually lived through its own virtues and goals. Hatred thrives on caricatures. Despite its religious concentration on the other, it is grievously removed and abstracted from the other in his being. Thus it is argued: let me discover my enemy as he truly is, and my hatred will subside.

This line of reasoning, however, fails to understand the real meaning of "differences" between human beings as they actually affect human relations. Differences between human beings are not the same thing as variant properties (such as color or size) in natural objects. What is "different" at the level of human encounter may confront a man as the "strange"; and it is well to remember that the word for stranger and the word for enemy in many languages is one and the same term. (The Latin word for example, is *hostis*.)

The figure of the stranger upsets the stable, familiar world that the preachers of tolerance presuppose. The stranger is not simply the person who is a variant of myself in certain specifiable ways. In fact, he stands outside the familiar world of comparisons and contrasts, variants and uniformities. That is why he is so hard to cope with—and tolerate. He arouses an uneasiness and aversion that passes quickly into fright and enmity. The experience is primordial. The stranger is the one who sends little boys scurrying behind their mothers' skirts when he leans over, grinning, to tell them what fine little fellows they are. Later in childhood, he is the object of mysterious parental warnings, as he is invested with a certain unspecified power to do harm. Strangers are tricky. Unlike everyone else they have no name. They are shadowy figures touched with a bit of menace. One would do well to give them a wide berth. And, still later, when strangers are multiplied by the thousands, they become "foreigners" whose arrival in a country in wave after wave is a shock to the nervous system of each subsequent generation. The experience of strangeness gives the lie to the assumption that beneath the hard mask of the enemy lies a familiar face, give or take a few wrinkles, as tolerable as my own. Actually I may find there the troubling face of the stranger for whose acceptance I am in no way prepared.

Nor does that more recent strategy of tolerance on the American scene—an easygoing friendliness of spirit—make a significant difference. The stranger does not dissolve in a grin under the impact of welcome wagons and newcomers' clubs, church guest registers and visitation committees, name cards at conventions and first-name bases. Who is the stranger? Surely he is not the newcomer who is easy prey to my friendliness. Rather, he is the man whom my friendliness fails to impress. Or again, he is the man whose friendliness toward me leaves me cold. The stranger is precisely the one who baffles me by refusing to wear the garment of humanity I offer him. The ideal of a tolerant friendliness of spirit is a little too fragile, a little too afraid to reckon with the stranger as he is, too easily discouraged, too quickly reduced to an expendable technique.

The doctrine of tolerance faces a further difficulty. Even if it could be demonstrated that underneath their differences all men are alike, it is not altogether clear that hatred would vanish forthwith. Unfortunately, it is possible to hate not only the threatening stranger but also those who are only too conspicuously like ourselves. Indeed, I may *already* be aware of the similarities between my foe and myself, and therefore condemn him. The difficulty is that hatred, like a goat, has the knack of devouring *everything*—virtues as well as vices, strengths as well as weaknesses, similarities as well as differences. It is not always true that hatred would vanish if we could only make people a little more aware of the good points of their foes.

Second, the ideal of tolerance includes a moral imperative based on its doctrine of man. Specifically it requires me to remove my enemy from the center to the periphery of my attention. I must let go of my religious obsession with him. Let him alone. Live and let live. Coexist. This is the spiritual advice of the preachers of tolerance. The obsession of anger with the past must be replaced by a willingness to forget; the obsession of suspicion with the future, by a willingness to overlook; the obses-

sion of resentment with a present reality, by a willingness to give
it a wide berth.

The only difficulty with this strategy is that the enemy is precisely the man whom I cannot remove from the center of my
consciousness. In hatred, the enemy occupies the foreground of
my life—whether he is my boss, my competitor, the New York
Jews, Castro, or the Anglo-Saxon Protestant. Moreover, even if
I were able, subjectively, to release him from the foreground to
the background of consciousness, it is my own honest conviction
that, objectively, my enemy would find his own way into the
foreground. "Give 'em an inch and they'll take a mile." Enemies
in the nature of the case are pushy. It is not we who hold them in
the foreground, but they who insist on occupying that place.

Despite these difficulties, however, we are not building an argument against the ideal of tolerance, as though this would serve
to promote the Christian faith on the subject of the enemy.
There is, after all, a certain truth to the plea to "live and let
live"; it ought not to be ignored. Moreover, certain events may
conceivably occur that make it psychologically possible for a person to overcome his religious obsessions with his enemy and to
refocus his life in such a way as to release a former enemy from
the pressure of suspicion and hostility. Finally, even if it could be
proved that tolerance as a solution is an inevitable failure, it
would be wrong to exploit this failure on the assumption that
the claims of the faith were thereby one whit stronger. The
foundations of Christian faith and life are not more secure for
being built over the rubble of other ethical systems.

Suffice it to say that the Christian response to the enemy is
basically different from the ideal of tolerance. Analysis and criticism of the ideal are useful, not in order to justify the faith, but
simply to understand it. The Christian response to the enemy is
distinctive both in its imperative and in the doctrine upon which
that imperative is based.

The command of love

Instead of relaxing one's attention in the manner of the tolerant, the imperative of the Christian faith requires an intensifying of focus upon the enemy. Consider the teachings of Jesus. He said, in effect: Does your enemy—the political leader you do not like, the colleague who irritates you—occupy a great deal of your attention? Do not try to solve your problem by driving him to the edge of your consciousness. Let him stand where he is. Now—love him. Love your enemies; bless them that curse you; pray for them that spitefully use and persecute you. Let your enemy stand before your eyes and let him be at the very center of your attention—the object of your concrete love, blessing, and intercessory prayer. This is the strange task given to the church, without the promise, moreover, that love will somehow disarm the enemy and turn him into the friend.

Clearly this imperative stands in sharpest contrast to the ideal of tolerance; yet it must not be supposed that ordinary, obsessive and possessive human love now becomes the pattern and substance of Christian love as opposed to tolerance. There is, after all, a certain releasing and letting go in Christian love, of which tolerance is a better analogue than human love. One thinks of the scriptural example of the adulterous woman (John 8:1–11), who is the center of an encircling and vengeful crowd, but whom the Lord releases from that circle with the words: "Let him who is without sin among you be the first to throw a stone at her." Interpreters of this passage have expended so much effort in showing that the Lord's act of forgiveness is distinct from the human act of indulgence or tolerance (which it is) that they fail to consider the distinctive impact of this event on the crowd. It is the Lord, after all, who forgives, not the crowd. The explosion of his judgment and forgiveness into the scene is such as to prompt the crowd simply to let the woman go. "But when they heard it, they went away, one by one. . . ." The encircling crowd can only break up and go away, as it surrenders the woman into the hands of the Lord. This is what we meant earlier by the element of truth in the ideal of tolerance.

Nevertheless, Christian moralists have always, and rightly, pointed out that Christian love differs basically from the ideal of tolerance. Tolerance is negative; love is positive. Christian love does not merely negate the obsessions of hatred with a vague benevolence. It calls for, in its own right, the peculiar focus of Christian love—that is, positive deeds of mercy and compassion directed toward the enemy and his good.

Jesus the enemy

There is nothing in Scripture comparable to the eighteenth-century assertion that all men, underneath the superficial garb of stranger or foe, are alike or nearly alike. The doctrine requires trimming and shaving away differences between men that are difficult to deny and that the biblical record itself accepts. Likewise there is nothing in Scripture comparable to the cosmopolitanism of the nineteenth and twentieth centuries, according to which men tolerate one another in their differences, either with the large-minded enthusiasm of the idealist or the aesthete, or with the superior, bemused air of the skeptic. Instead, the command to love the enemy rests on the astonishing assertion that God himself has come as the enemy. God requires men to love the enemy because he has first loved men and come to them under this very form. For the Christian, this identification is unmistakable: Jesus is the enemy; he is the implacable foe.

If I am out on the prowl in my sin, who would I least want to catch me out? My wife? My boss? Perhaps so. But both may be susceptible to blandishment. It might be possible, for a variety of reasons, to keep them from doing their worst or to survive their worst when done. But who is really my implacable foe? My incorruptible foe? My unimpressionable and disinterested foe? Who is the one who, in truth, I would least want to ambush me when I am attending to one of my devious adventures? God is the one whose existence unassailably prevents me from being the man I want to be.

The familiar language of the Old and New Testaments on the subject of enmity should be re-examined in this perspective. Beginning with the Prophets and continuing with the poet of Lamentations, the Word of salvation comes as a declaration of war:

> How the Lord in his anger
> has set the daughter of Zion under a cloud!
>
> .   .   .   .
>
> He has bent his bow like an enemy,
> with his right hand set like a foe;
> and he has slain all the pride of our eyes
> in the tent of the daughter of Zion;
> he has poured out his fury like fire.
>
> Lamentations 2:1, 4

Nothing in the New Testament softens up this opposition between God and man. Jesus is the enemy of his people. He is a threat to their religion (a "blasphemer") and a threat to their morality, for he forgives sins. His righteous death is a judgment on the unrighteousness of the people, and his death among the unrighteous, a judgment upon the self-righteousness of the people. Golgotha is a battleground. For this reason, the Christian faith has described a confrontation with the Savior as nothing less than a crucifixion—from both sides. Through enmity toward him, men put him to death, but through his love he puts them to death, that they may be raised from the dead, wholly new in him. The Crucifixion at the center of Christian worship makes it impossible for the Christian to think of the command to love the enemy as a disturbing ethical afterthought to an otherwise peaceful religious relationship. The enemy already stands before him in worship itself. In fact, the worshipper does not really know Jesus unless he knows Jesus as his enemy and unless he knows himself as Jesus' enemy. Moreover, the Resurrection of Jesus does not change this situation. It only intensifies it. The body of the risen Lord continues to bear the marks of his crucifixion. It reminds the Christian that God's new life stands in full contradiction to his old life and to his deadness in that life. God's life means an end to his old life in sin. The Resurrection, no less than the Crucifixion, defines a conflict between God and man.

God's identification with the form of the enemy has important consequences for the love-command, but a question blocks the way. How can one speak in any meaningful sense of God's identification with the enemy, when the word "enemy" is used in two different ways: with reference to the relationships between God and man, and to those between human foes? Human enemies oppose one another, after all, for the purpose of bringing evil upon each other; whereas God opposes men to bring them to their good. God is hostile to man only as sinner; whereas men are hostile to each other as creatures, whether or not they sin. Is it not equivocation, therefore, to speak of God's identification with the enemy when the term is restricted and softened as applied to God? Would it not be better to concede a certain metaphorical significance in its application to God but refrain from forcing it to carry a weight in the ethics of love that it cannot bear?

Two considerations are in order by way of reply. First, although the term "enemy" is applied in differing ways to God and to man, this difference ought not to discourage the Christian moralist from drawing certain ethical implications from the use of the one term in both cases. After all, no term applied both to God and to man is free of a certain double or analogical meaning —whether father, judge, husband, or king. Yet the fact of double meaning has never prevented the Christian moralist from recognizing the profound ethical implications contained in the use of a single term. The use of the word "father" with respect to God and to certain men not only discloses something about God but also illuminates men's responsibilities to their earthly fathers. The use of the term "enemy" with respect to God may have not only a theological value, as it discloses something about God, but also a moral value, as it illuminates the Christian's responsibilities to his earthly enemies.

Second, although there is a distinction between the two meanings of the term "enemy," the distinction is not such as to imply a more attenuated meaning in its application to God. Quite the contrary, the term "enmity" has its strongest meaning in its application to God. Human enemies, after all, learn how to bargain with one another on the sly. Foreign ministers may meet in neutral embassies, or foot soldiers exchange an occasional courtesy. But the opposition between God and the sinner is radical, total, and nonnegotiable. That is why the believer has always looked upon Christian conversion as a more comprehensive and radical event than the acceptance of capitalism by the Communist or of communism by the capitalist. The conflicts and polarities between men pale in comparison with the conflict between God and men. If there is a distinction between the two meanings of "enmity," therefore, it is that the very power and strength of its application to God relativizes its import among men as an excuse for sin.

It must be admitted that moralists interpreting the Christian tradition have not usually connected the command to love the enemy with God's own identification as the enemy. It is usually asserted that God, in addition to loving us, loves those who are our enemies. For this reason, we must also love our enemies. God's love extends not only to the just but to the unjust, not only to those whom we appreciate but to those whom we despise. Therefore we must follow after God, so to speak, pursuing, in love, our foes.

There is no need to contest the truth in this line of teaching. The command to love is rooted, after all, in love! But unless the command to love is rooted in God's enmity just as surely as in his love, it is subject to two disastrous falsifications. The Christian may lapse into either condescension or despair. First, when Christians occupy the place of the just praying for the unjust, they are tempted to condescension. They pray—and love—with that dangerous hypocrisy that used to infect Christian prayers for the Jews (as though they alone were God's enemy). Precisely this condescension is forbidden to the Christian in the discovery that God is his enemy and that he is God's enemy. Less often mentioned, however, is the second temptation to despair. When the Christian follows conscientiously after the exemplary love of God, he cannot fail to note with dismay that his own love thins out as it leaves the circle of his friends. Not surprisingly, he grows less and less convinced of God's love for the foe, undermined as he is by the collapse of his own. He has no firsthand experience of that love that would contradict his own sense of love's failure to reach the foe—except that he knows God's love for him as a love for the foe. It is extraordinarily important, therefore, to begin where Scripture begins, not only with God's love of the enemy but also with God's love *as the enemy,* a love by which the Christian himself is judged and encouraged.

There are at least two further consequences for Christian behavior that must be drawn from the fact that God comes to the Christian himself under the form of the enemy. First, the Christian is relieved of every objective ground for paranoia. "If God is for us, who is against us?" (Romans 8:31) If God has brought forward every serious accusation against a man in the course of his salvation, then no further charge remains that can imperil his life and destiny in God. The enemy has been relativized. He is no longer an ultimate threat. The skies, the sea, and the land have been swept clean of every force as a final power of destruction. Satan has fallen like lightning from the heavens. Nothing else remains to threaten the creature before God. This is the metaphysical context in which men are permitted to live and breathe. It is the sum and substance of Romans 8.

If the enemy has been relativized, so man's response to his human enemies has been placed under a fundamental limitation and restraint. If God comes under the form of the enemy, the Christian cannot relate to his enemy as though he is godless. There is nothing more confused, pitiful, or self-righteous from the lips of a Christian than the phrase, "the godless atheist," as though God exists and morality applies only among those who belong to the God Worshipers' Club. If God exists, then no man is godless, especially not one's enemies, because God recovers men for life with himself under this baffling form. For good political reasons a man may feel called upon to vote against his enemies. In extremity, for just reasons, he may feel compelled to meet force with counterforce, but he can do neither as though the enemy belongs to the devil. This is a satanism which was destroyed once and for all in the Cross.

6 The Sin Against the Needy:
NEGLECT

Sins against the needy are, in an important sense, the exact opposite of those against the enemy. The enemy occupies the center of attention; he becomes an obsession. But the needy, at the other extreme, barely exists. He camps out at the very perimeter of consciousness. If he claims our attention, he does so only fleetingly, when the doorbell rings on the day of the Community Chest drive or when the mail brings, somewhat disappointingly, not the letter from the friend we expect but a reminder of the cause we would ignore. Sin, in this case, is not a matter of obsession but of indifference and neglect. The needy is someone whose world we do not choose to enter. We find the very thought of it too depressing, his exigencies too unbearable. So we develop ways of turning him aside, of seeing him without seeing, of answering him without hearing, of building our superhighways, smooth and efficient, so as to by-pass his particular section of town.

Jesus' parables of the Good Samaritan and the Last Judgment are the classic passages on this form of sin. The priest and the Levite on the road to Jericho are not men whose sin involves hostility. Nothing suggests that they are more than ordinary careerists, too heavily pressed for time to stop and pay attention. In order to avoid any awkwardnesses, therefore, they tactfully "passed along on the other side." It is as though they saw their own world about to collide with another that was messy and potentially fraught with inconvenience and delay; they decided to take marginal note of this second world, some fifty yards ahead, and, with professional grace, step aside.

The strategies of the sin of oversight remain much the same

to this day—except that the act of stepping aside has become a device of the community itself. It is not that men are more cruelly indifferent to their fellows than in times past but that they have learned how to naturalize the sins of oversight in the context of an urban society. The notorious neglect of the neighbor that characterizes the behavior of the modern city dweller reflects a social style which, under the impersonal, anonymous conditions of urban life, seems wholly natural. If a man who knows my name ignores me, his act is somewhat deliberate; in a sense he has to defy the world by rendering someone he knows invisible and inaudible. But if a man for whom I am one of a nameless multitude ignores me, he merely appears to be taking the world as it comes. His neglect seems natural.

Not only does urban anonymity degrade the needy by making them nameless, it also inspires in the affluent a social style excessively concerned with self-advertisement. Each becomes his own aggressive publicity agent in order to overcome his anonymity. The emphasis falls on being seen and being heard rather than on seeing and hearing others in the nuances of their real needs.

Our society has even learned how to remove the needy from sight in the very act of serving them. There is no need to step around the afflicted. We have developed an efficient ambulance service that removes them from sight with the speed of violence itself. No one should ignore the humanitarian gain in modern techniques; in comparison, the Good Samaritan was a rank amateur at first aid. But who can deny the less savory advantages in our efficiency? We provide the needy with certain social services (not enough), but we protect ourselves thereby from distracting, personal contacts with them. We have learned how to remove from sight the sick, the aged, the dying, the poor, the malformed, and war cripples; we seal them off in parts of town through which we never travel, or assign them to institutions we never enter. Behind our public world of skyscrapers, expressways, and suburban ease remains a hidden world of need.*

---

* Michael Harrington's book *The Other America* (New York: Macmillan, 1963), pointed out that there are fifty million poor people in America, a scarcely credible figure, precisely because poverty, while real, has become increasingly invisible in the United States.

Occasionally the ugliness of neglect becomes apparent. The body of a lonely man who has died in his room is discovered when it begins to stink. A woman dies at the hands of a murderer because her cries fail to inspire even one of her forty neighbors to phone the police. Suddenly a generation of alienated minorities growing up in our northern cities begins to stir. The needy momentarily and dramatically intrude themselves into the national consciousness, and a war on poverty is declared. In fact, the needy become a "Cause." But then, in the very moment of success, the ingredients of neglect take hold. The Cause develops its professionals, its patrons, and its yearly budget. Legislation is passed. Interest flags. The sufferers themselves fade from sight behind the institutions and slogans that serve them. And so, once a year, publicity agents must be hired to bring out specimens of affliction, in order to renew some sense of their concrete existence and their claim upon our attention.

Every effort on behalf of the needy is an effort to get attention. The diseased must make their yearly appearances before television cameras in order to overcome their invisibility behind the statistical abstraction of the Cause. The Negro must take to the streets. He must engage in "demonstrations." He has to be seen if his campaign for equal rights is not to die of neglect.

Although it does not seem so on the surface, there is something even more dehumanizing and degrading about sins born of neglect than those born of hatred. In hatred, the enemy has our attention. We may have a somewhat abstract view of him, but at least he exists. The neglected man has no such status. The present spiritual crisis in America over the race issue bears this out. Moderate whites have wondered why Negroes have been so "reckless" in the pursuit of their goals, perhaps endangering their very achievement. But the fact is that the Negro, who never succeeded in getting the white man's attention as a man in need, has been able to get it by seriously threatening to become his enemy. This represents, though negatively, the attainment of some status as a human being.

Most men do not take the sins of oversight as seriously as they do the sins of malice; there is an assumption of innocence, or near-innocence, in the case of neglect. "We did not think to help

so and so. We were simply preoccupied. But now that we know of
his plight, of course we will help." There is an informal assumption here of the following scale of seriousness in the social sins,
reading from the venial to the deadly: innocent oversight, culpa-
ble neglect, and malicious harm.

In a sense this ranking of the three sins is just, but there are
certain occasions in which the position of the first two in respect
to the third must be reversed. Our mild and somewhat self-
pitying terms for excusing ourselves as "busy," "pressed for
time," "preoccupied"—the very terms used to prove the innocence of our oversights—are often simply euphemisms for describing the worst of the soul's ailments—occlusion. The occluded man is shut off from others. Far from being innocent, he
has actually arrived at the final destination toward which those
who hate their enemies aspire. For it is the goal of the man
who truly hates his enemy to see his enemy utterly destroyed,
leaving himself in sole possession of his world. This, the ultimate
destination of hatred, is but the place where some men who are
too busy to notice their neighbors begin. From the very outset,
the neighbor does not exist for them. As mild and harmless as it
may appear, their self-engrossment is but man's inhumanity to
man brought to its perfection in pride: the sin of solitary self-
love.

But what is the self-engrossment of which the neglectful are
guilty? Here it is only too easy to overlook the real predicament
of the neglectful, by missing the truth on which the sin feeds.
Most sermons on the subject assume that people are neglectful
because they are rich, smug, and self-satisfied. The priest and
Levite are presented, accordingly, as assured, successful, and
complacent men of affairs who sweep along the road to Jericho
altogether too busy to turn aside. Caricatured in this way, the
neglectful are restricted to the villainous rich, those who are
absorbed in their own successful enterprises. This caricature
leaves others free to offer excuses for their neglect, based on their
sense of their own neediness and poverty.

It is well, then, to consider the excuses of neglect. They blurt
out their own truth. They sometimes reveal only too accurately
not smugness but anxiety, not self-assurance but despair. The

statement, "I am too busy," may simply be a way of saying in anxiety, "I am riddled with concern about my own affairs. I can't break free from the grip of my own needs. They hold me in a vise. Maybe next year will be different. But this year is impossible." Or again the question, "What can I do?" may only be a way of saying in despair, "I have nothing for the other's real needs because what I have doesn't satisfy my own. What use could I possibly be to him? It is better to avoid him. To have to face him would be too depressing. He would remind me of my own poverty." Many a man dreads—or avoids altogether—a visit to the home of a dying friend for reason of the latter despair. He knows he has nothing to say that will help. He is not rich and complacent; he is bankrupt before his friend's imminent death and his own. Such a man is in need himself. He is less the priest or the Levite of traditional fame than the stricken traveler on the side of the road. He knows, however obscurely, that he himself needs a savior. This is a truth about neglect that those who are too assured in their philanthropies sometimes ignore.

The ideal of philanthropy and Christian love of the needy

If man's chief resource against the hatred of the enemy has been the ideal of tolerance, his chief resource against neglect is the ideal of philanthropy. Mere toleration of the needy is not enough; alone, it is intolerable. The afflicted need positive acts of help. Philanthropy at its best inspires such help—and not simply at the level of episodic personal charity, but also in persistent efforts to construct a just society where needs are sensitively met.

There is no reason to depreciate the philanthropist in order to commend the Christian faith on the subject of the needy. The man of good works, however, does face a serious temptation: condescension. He is tempted to play the role of savior to the have-nots—whether he crudely expects a fulsome gratitude and praise for his good works, or whether he reserves for himself the more delicate pleasures of anonymous giving. Incontestably, condescension is destructive of human community. It is absolutely fatal in the attitude of a speaker to his audience, a doctor to his patient; and it is certainly no less poisonous in the life of the church, whenever her service in the world is a barely concealed condescension. No man is quite so tone deaf to things of the spirit as not to be aware when another man is condescending to him.

The Christian is forbidden condescension toward the needy, first, because he cannot serve the needy without recognizing his own radical need before God; all subjective grounds for condescension are thereby removed. Second, and equally important: the Lord who occupies the center of attention of the believing church is the one who identified himself in the form of the needy. He suffered, thirsted, and died in the radical poverty of the Cross. "Though he was rich, yet for your sake he became poor. . . ." (II Corinthians 8:9) Therefore, all objective grounds for condescension are removed. It is impossible to take this God seriously and then to assign the needy a place on the periphery of vision or on a level below believers. To condescend to the needy is nothing short of blasphemy: it is to condescend to God.

Scripture offers powerful warrant for this perspective. First, condescension is forbidden by virtue of a man's own self-placement in need before God. In the Old Testament the Lord commands the people of Israel, in harvesting their crops, to leave some grain for the sojourner for "you were once sojourners in Egypt." The very basis for God's command to attend to the needy is the event of his gracious dealing with Israel in her need. Therefore, the people cannot receive this command from a promontory from which they look down upon the poor. The command takes hold of them by enlivening the memory of their dependence upon God's grace. So also, the Savior of the New Testament summons men to attend to the needs of others, as they themselves have been attended to. A fresh and persuasive exegesis of the Parable of the Good Samaritan supports this view.

* For what follows, see Karl Barth, *Church Dogmatics*, ed. G. W. Bromiley and T. F. Torrance (12 Vols.; Edinburgh: T. & T. Clark, 1956), Vol. I, Pt. II, pp. 417–419. It should be added that this elucidation is unusual only in our own day. It was at one time the tradition of the church.

It has usually been assumed that the parable is a simple homily summoning the disciple to good deeds. Thus the hearer should begin by identifying himself with the priest and the Levite, convicted of the sin of neglect; and then he should proceed by imitating the good example of the Samaritan, attentive to the neighbor in his need. Within the limits of this interpretation, the hearer does not identify himself with the stricken traveler in the story. This role is reserved for war orphans, widows, the poor, the starving, and the diseased—those whom Jesus, by means of the story, calls upon the disciple to serve. Within these limits, the hearer does not have to confront the Samaritan himself (not, at least, accept him as his own helper—only as a moral example by which he is judged). Within these limits, in other words, the story fails to establish what its context makes clear is intended: the need of the hearer himself for the Savior-Samaritan's works of love.

This focus is clear when we recall that Jesus offers the story in a discussion of the command to love the neighbor. Specifically, a lawyer pressed him with the question: "And who is *my* neighbor?" It is often assumed that the answer to this question is: "The man who fell among thieves." But when, at the end of his parable, Jesus asks, "Which of these three, do you think, proved neighbor to the man who fell among the robbers?" the lawyer answers quite properly, "The one who showed mercy on him" (Luke 10:36–37). Thus the story begins: Who is my neighbor? (whom I should love); and the story ends: My neighbor is the one who has shown mercy to me, the savior who touches me with a mercy that sets me on my feet and sends me on my way. This is the one I am called to love. The only question remaining is implied at the end of the story: How do I love the savior who has shown compassion to me? And the answer is given: Go and do likewise.

The story makes it impossible to put on airs in dealing with the needy. The only needy person introduced until the very end of the story is the listener himself. Far from blurring a Christian concern with the needy, the effect of the parable should be to sharpen a focus upon them. Every basis for condescension in an exalted notion of one's self is undercut. To look over men from a height above them has become preposterous.

Condescension toward the neighbor is forbidden for the second reason: God has identified himself with the needy. By implication, then, to neglect or to condescend to the needy is to neglect or to condescend to God. But who are the needy in this case? There is the spiritual sense of the term (that tends to dominate the reinterpretation of the parable of the Good Samaritan): the neediness of every man before God; and a material sense: the need of the poor for bread, clothing, and shelter. In this second sense, the term refers to those who are insignificant and powerless in the eyes of the world. Both meanings are intended in Scripture. But there is no doubt that the second has a primacy in Scripture as that special identification which God himself chooses and which acts as a sign of God's judgment and promise with respect to the first.

In the Old Testament it is clear that God sees and hears and identifies himself with the cause of the poor and the powerless. As if to emphasize this point, there are repeated references to the widow, the orphan, and the sojourner—that is, to those individuals who had no direct voice in ancient courts of law and therefore could not draw attention to themselves. God identifies himself with people who, from the worldly point of view, are invisible and inaudible. In the New Testament, Jesus makes this identification final and decisive. "Truly, I say to you, as you did it to one of the least of these my brethren, you did it to me" (Matthew 25:40). No passage makes it clearer that the command to love the needy is not an ethical afterthought in the Christian life. The Lord takes those who fade into the distant reaches of consciousness in the ordinary course of life (the hungry, the thirsty, the stranger, the naked, the sick, and the imprisoned), and he recovers them for the very center of attention before the judgment seat. More prominent on the day of Judgment than the commands, you shall not steal and you shall not kill, is the command, you shall not ignore.

As impressive, however, as the content of Jesus' teaching on the Last Judgment is its placement in the Gospel narrative. The teaching that appears in Matthew 25 is followed immediately by the decisive events in which his own promised identification with the needy is brought to its completion in his suffering and death. "When Jesus had finished all these sayings, he said to his disciples, 'You know that after two days the Passover is coming, and the Son of man will be delivered up to be crucified'" (Matthew 26:1–2). The solidarity of Christ with the thirsty, the imprisoned, and the naked is promptly lived out. He suffers arrest, like those in prison; he is stripped of his clothes and scourged; and he dies thirsty among thieves on a cross. The Son of man no longer teaches men about the terms and conditions of his future coming. He confronts men with the command to love under the mute form of his own flesh.

7 The Sin Against the Friend: BETRAYAL

After World War II, the question arose as to whether William Joyce, the notorious "Lord Haw-Haw," could legitimately be tried for treason for his broadcasting on behalf of the Nazis during the war. Although Joyce had lived with his family in the British Isles since early childhood, neither he nor his family had ever applied for British papers. Born in Brooklyn, New York, he was still, formally considered, an American citizen. Eventually, of course, Joyce was prosecuted and hung, on the basis of principles which have determined the definition of treason since the sixteenth century. Sir Edward Coke (1552–1634), the eminent English jurist, had summarized these principles with the phrase: "Protection draws allegiance and allegiance draws protection." Joyce had accepted and enjoyed the protection of the British crown. Whatever his formal status as a citizen, he owed the British government his loyalty.

Quite apart from its application in Joyce's case, Coke's principle offers a model for a theological understanding of treason. Men owe their very existence and well-being to God. Apart from him, they would vanish into nothing. The creature belongs wholly to God and to God alone. The protection that God offers, moreover, is not a general sort of protection proffered from a distance. In redeeming men, he shared the very substance of his life with them in the person of his son. He extended himself toward men in the way that no country could afford to: he died for them. This fact is touchingly clear in the rites attendant to a military funeral. The casket of a soldier is draped with his country's flag, but when the coffin is about to be lowered into the ground, the flag is neatly folded and withdrawn. At the last moment, if you will, it betrays him. A man may die for his country, but the country does not die for the man.

The protection of God is subject to no such limit. This is at the center of Christian affirmation. God went down into the grave, where no flag can go. This is the significance of the three days in which Jesus lay in the grave. They describe the downward movement from God to man brought to its completion in Jesus' death. The dignity of a flag does not permit its burial, but the majesty of God is consummated in desecration. As the creed puts it, for our sake he "Suffered under Pontius Pilate; was crucified, dead and buried." In the course of this movement into the grave, God places himself in absolute solidarity with each man. He takes upon himself that extremity before which human community is forced to withdraw, the extremity of death, and he absorbs it in his own person. He remains faithful to men in this event, even though they have put him to death. The protection of God so offered is the faithfulness of God. He is faithful in mercy, faithful in judgment, faithful in patience with man's stupidity, inhumanity, heroism, weakness, disloyalty, and shame. God became man, and he has not, and he will not desert him. Unreserved protection deserves unreserved loyalty.

Treason in this theological context is a failure to grant to God unconditional loyalty. Thus, it is the generic feature of all sin rather than the specific sin of political treason or personal betrayal. All sins are treasonous in character and not just the specific sin of political treason or personal betrayal. A man may fail to be loyal to God through acts of political treason, but may fail equally by an idolatrous attitude toward the state. He may fail to be loyal to God when he betrays another person, but equally by a slavish devotion to an authoritarian personality.

The distinction between the generic feature of all sin and the specific sins of political treason and personal betrayal must be reaffirmed at the outset of this essay. The fact that all sin is treason against God does not mean that all activities legally defined as treasonous are in fact sinful or that when they are sinful they, alone, are sin. Indeed, precisely because all sin is treasonous, not all political treason can be characterized as sin. Unconditional loyalty to God means that loyalty to a particular country, government, or party can never be unconditional. Admittedly, loyalty to God inspires and requires loyalty to one's fellow creatures, whom God created and whose life he shares. But, at the same time, it forbids an idolatrous obedience to the state. Normally, Christian criticism of the state should take place within the bounds of loyalty. But circumstances are at least conceivable, dreadful though they may be, when it would be impossible to continue loyal to God and to one's people except through activity, which, legally defined, is treasonous.

These limiting comments on the specific sin of treason are particularly important in the age of the totalitarian state. Under the conditions of a totalitarian society, treason and treason alone is the cardinal sin. Moreover, it is a sin that a paranoid government is likely to see everywhere. Dictators (and Birchite superpatriots in nervous democracies) are notoriously free with their accusations of treason. They are prone to identify the traitor as any and all their opponents. The concept of Her Majesty's loyal opposition disappears altogether. It must not be forgotten that more crimes have been committed in the twentieth century by man against man in the name of duty than have been perpetrated by those guilty of legally defined treason.

And yet the seriousness of the specific sin of treason cannot be denied. Dante reserves the innermost circle of hell for those who

are guilty of treason. There he has placed Judas, Brutus, and
Cassius—the most notorious of traitors—in the three mouths of
Satan himself. Revealingly, the poet does not rely on the image
of fire for his description of their plight. The souls of traitors are
held fast in a lake of ice. Clearly, the worst of sins against the
brother are those of the frozen heart. Those who are disloyal to
others have chosen a life isolated and immobile, a life, in effect,
hostile to life, for which the only adequate image is a sunless
waste of ice.

In Dante's society, of course, public treason and personal betrayal were not clearly distinguished. Loyalty to the state was,
interchangeably, a personal loyalty to one's own master, king, or
lord. Allegiance focused, publicly as well as privately, in a
person, and, most usually, in a person who filled an office superior to one's own. As such, betrayal was not, as we have called it,
the sin against the friend; more typically, it was the sin against
the master, liege, or lord.

In contemporary American society, the shape of the spiritual
problem of loyalty has both changed and intensified. It has
changed, in that public treason and personal betrayal are more
distinct from one another than in the distant past. Public treason
is an impersonal act directed against the national state. Betrayal
of the person, meanwhile, is a private act, directed, most typically,
not against those superior to oneself but against one's equals. In
equalitarian America, betrayal is one of the most troubling—and
yet unexamined—of sins, directed, most typically, against one's
friends.

Not since Josiah Royce, however, has the problem of personal
loyalty and disloyalty received much attention from American
moralists. This oversight has its own serious consequences, not
the least of which is the tendency of people to be especially self-
righteous toward those accused, or found guilty, of political disloyalty. The fury of a nation toward its traitors, real and
imagined, may reflect not simply the seriousness of the crime but
also men's uneasiness toward their own daily, but unexamined,
treasons.

Personal betrayal and the American ideal of friendliness

Americans carry a heavy burden of guilt for the sin of personal betrayal. This spiritual problem has intensified, because Americans are caught in the pressures of a double system. On the one hand, they experience the pressure of a social system that is highly professional, bureaucratic, and competitive—energized throughout by the rewards of promotion. On the other hand, they experience the pressure of a social style which is based on an ideal of friendship. Whereas the social structure is impersonal, increasingly hierarchical, and competitive, the social style is personal, equalitarian, and helpful. The resultant moral conflicts between style and system are immense.

Some societies protect their members from such conflicts by separating the public order of work from the private order of friendship. But Americans peculiarly combine these orders at the risk of straining and corrupting them both. Friendships sour in competitive situations, and professional decisions become distorted through personal involvements. The reason for this tension lies in the American commitment to friendliness as a social ideal. It is difficult for Americans to surrender their style on behalf of an impersonal obedience to a social system. However debased the ideal of friendliness may have become in our own time, a powerful religious yearning lies at its root.

The American yearning for friendship is mystical in its temper, but this does not mean that it is particularly profound. Indeed, Europeans find the American experience of friendship rather superficial. Its superficiality, however, may be related to the intensity with which Americans strain after immediacy with each other. Just as the mystic, for the sake of immediacy with God, seeks to overcome the distinctions between God and himself that creatureliness imposes, so the American seeks to annul, through friendliness, the distinctions that different origins, memories, hopes, and talents may involve. The terms in the equation are hardly proportionate, but the quest for immediacy in each case justifies the comparison. Both the mystic and the American prefer the direct to the indirect, the immediate to the mediated; they would annihilate distinctions of time, space, and position for the sake of a direct breakthrough in the moment. It is pointless to dwell upon the historical origins and development of this ideal and style in the successive contexts of the frontier, the small town, the overcrowded cities, and the postwar suburbs. Whatever its history, the important point is the degree to which the American social style depends upon immediate contacts between people, without barriers or reserve.

Caught between the demands of an impersonal social system and a social style in which friendliness counts for so much, the American moves in two directions at once. He makes an effort to be friends with everybody, but then finds himself involved in making professional judgments and decisions about those with whom he has made friends. The intimacies of friendship are such as to inspire some measure of personal loyalty, but they also render two people more vulnerable to each other in their weaknesses than they might ordinarily be. A man suddenly finds himself deliberating impersonally about those in whom he has confided and who have confided in him. He is uncomfortably involved in turning them over to the machinery of the system— without being entirely certain that the system itself hands out justice as it reviews the individual case.

The intense competitiveness of the system exacerbates the situation by its lack of a ceiling above and a floor below. The rewards for backbiting can be tempting; the threat of betrayal by others, chilling. Under these pressures, the social style remains outwardly friendly and direct, but inwardly a certain wariness and suspicion takes possession of the soul. No longer does the social style express and serve the quest for immediacy. Friendliness becomes a format behind which a person operates, exploiting its advantages where he can.

The damage caused by betrayal is not simply the specific consequence of a given deed for which a man feels guilty but the deterioration of the order of friendship as a whole. The social style now transmits signals that no one can wholly trust. Friendship itself is no longer nourishing. The show of friendliness—the "sincere manner"—may invite comradeship while simultaneously warding it off. It seeks to purchase confidences cheaply without paying the price in loyalty. A capacity for friendship means a capacity for discipline which a promiscuous social style works to undermine.

Betrayal defined

Every act of betrayal—whether public or private—involves a very simple triad: the betrayer, the betrayed, and the enemy. In its primary form, the sin may be defined as a deed whereby we deliver into the hands of the enemy those who have placed themselves trustingly into our hands. This definition is guided by the literal meaning of the Latin root for the terms "betrayal" and "treason." *Tradere* means to "hand over, to hand on, to deliver, hence to betray."* The Greek word for betray (*paradidomi*) also means literally to hand over or to deliver over. Thus in the passion narrative it is recorded: ". . . the Son of man will be delivered to the chief priests and scribes, and they will condemn him to death, and deliver him to the Gentiles. . . ." (Matthew 20:18–19) Or again: ". . . the Son of man is betrayed into the hands of sinners" Matthew 26:45). The basic mechanism of treason is written into the language of Scripture itself, and it consists of the following four elements: first, it is an *act*; second, it is the act of *handing over*; third, it is the act of handing over the *friend*; fourth and finally, it is the act of handing over the friend *into the hands of the enemy*.

Judas' betrayal of Jesus determines this definition of treason. Judas hands over Jesus, who had placed himself into the hands of his disciples, into the hands of the high priests. Therewith he sets in motion a whole series of further acts. The high priests hand Jesus over to the Roman authorities, who in turn hand him over to the crowds, who in turn give him over to condemnation and death. When Judas saw what he had done, he took his life with

* Eric Patridge, *Origins: A Short Etymological Dictionary of Modern English* (3rd ed.; London: Routledge & Kegan Paul, 1961), p. 733.

his own hands because there was no way to recover or to cover over the consequences of his act.

First, the sin of betrayal is an act. It is more than a mere passion or wish. In this respect it differs from the traditional seven capital sins, which, as we have seen, were defined more directly by a ruling passion. The sin of envy, for example, need be nothing more than an interior passion to be itself. The envious man, first and foremost, *feels* something. He may subsequently go on to do his neighbor harm, but such an act is not itself envy. The traitor, however, by definition, has proceeded to an action. He does something on the basis of his passions, whatever they may be. There are Judas' kiss, Peter's denial, and the high priests' accusations—all of them responsible deeds. ". . . Out of envy . . . they had delivered him up. . . ." (Matthew 27:18) The traitor's act need not, of course, always take the form of overt action. If he is clever enough, he may know how to betray another by maintaining silence at a critical moment or by letting the faintest of smiles pass across his face. Soundless desertion, just as effectively as the loudest of accusations, may surrender the neighbor defenseless into the hands of the enemy.

Occasionally, the fact that betrayal is an act may be obscured by virtue of its incessant repetition, if betrayal becomes a style of life. One no longer makes a discrete decision to betray a particular person; betrayal has become a pattern of behavior in which one is disloyal to others almost aimlessly and continually. The secrets and weaknesses of friends are readily surrendered in social chatter wholly undisciplined by loyalty; they seem such a trifle to pay for the delicious intimacy that comes while warming hands over the fire of someone else's reputation. Under these circumstances, betrayal may be so deeply written into social behavior that it no longer impresses the conscience with the enormity of an isolated action.

Second, betrayal consists of the specific act of "handing over." There is an element of violence implied. In betrayal one lays hold of the power or the sovereignty of another (whether it be the freedom of a subject or the sovereignty of a nation) and delivers it, so bound, into the hands of a third party. The traitor binds the sovereignty of his country by surrendering its secrets, and therewith its strength, to a foreign power. Delilah takes advantage of intimacies with Samson to deliver him weakened into the hands of the Philistines. Underlings exploit their knowledge of peers to deliver them compromised into the hands of the boss. A child reports on her younger brother in order to enjoy his suffering at the hands of higher power. Adam hands Eve over to God, judged and condemned, as the cause of his sin.

Dante showed a precise knowledge of this element in treason. In the *Inferno* he contrasts several partners in sin as they react when met by Vergil and himself. Francesca, guilty of the sin of lust, remains loyal to her partner, Paolo, by excusing him. Ulysses, guilty of the sin of fraud, ignores his partner. But Ugolino, guilty of the sin of treason, quite characteristically denounces his partner to every passer-by.*

The device of handing over is no less evident in those who are guilty of self-betrayal. Self-betrayers are seldom so comfortable as when they are busy denouncing themselves to others. They hand themselves over, judged and condemned, by their own gestures and words. One thinks of the plight of the schoolboy forced to make his first public speech. He is tempted to betray himself by making faces at his own mistakes. Somewhat pathetically, the schoolboy speaker is delivered over by himself, the schoolboy critic, into the hands of his critical peers. Unable to stand his ground against the enemy, he makes the desperate attempt to join them at his own expense. Ludicrous in boyhood, such ploys in self-betrayal can be savage and relentless in adult life.

Third, the betrayer hands over those who, in some respect, have placed themselves in his hands. For this reason we have called it the peculiar sin against the friend. Friendship involves mutual self-disclosure: the exchanges of confidences and gifts. In friendship a man shares and entrusts himself to another to some degree. Given this advantage, the traitor does not have to mount a direct assault on the power of another, in the fashion of an enemy. His victim has already placed himself, vulnerable, into

* Cf. *Dante's Inferno*, trans. John D. Sinclair (New York: Oxford, 1961), esp. Mr. Sinclair's comments, p. 415.

his hands. He can take advantage of the freedom of movement that friendship gives him. He is in a position to seize power at a critical point by exploiting trust and love. The enemy clamors at the door from without; the traitor opens the door from within.*

Once again, Dante shows special sensitivity to this aspect of treason. In the *Inferno* he is particularly severe on those guilty of breaches in the laws of hospitality. To deal badly with a guest is to betray someone who has placed himself in your hands. (Macbeth's crime against his king is surely compounded by the fact that Duncan is a guest in his house.) Likewise, to deal badly with a host is to betray someone who has made himself vulnerable by opening up his house. Not often, of course, do modern men take violent advantage of such opportunities. It is more likely that they will exploit the intimacies provided by the relationships of guest-host, host-guest for the more civilized betrayals of gossip.

Fourth, the traitor lays hands on someone with the final aim of handing him over to the enemy. He intends evil for his victim. In betrayal at its worst, the enemy into whose hands he hopes to surrender his victim is Satan. Although he surrenders his victim directly into the hands of other powers—mother, policeman, peers, teacher, judge, a foreign power, or God—he actually hopes that one of these agents will function as the instrument of Satan —that is, will punish, humiliate, confuse, or destroy.

The traitor, however, may not always be so resolutely malicious in his intention. He may not hope for total destruction. He may even be convinced that he accomplishes a certain good by his actions. In these cases, it is well to be reminded that betrayal has a way of producing results beyond one's reach. It trips off a mechanism over which one has no control. The traitor catapults his victim into the hands of those whose zest for violence may be

---

* Obviously, a country does not make itself vulnerable in the hands of its citizens in the same way and degree to which this is done in friendship. Nevertheless the citizen—if for no other reason than the protective coloration he enjoys of common language, appearance, and experience—has a potential power over his fellow citizens that the alien does not enjoy.

more savage than he intended. I may report something on a competitor, only wanting to see him cut down to size, but I may live to see him get cut to ribbons. The fact that I have not chosen these consequences in detail does not blunt my responsibility for this action. As a traitor, my spectacular success—the overkill, as it were, in my action—may be my most excruciating punishment. "When Judas, his betrayer, saw that he was condemned, he repented and brought back the thirty pieces of silver to the chief priests and the elders, saying, 'I have sinned in betraying innocent blood.' They said, 'What is that to us? See to it yourself'" (Matthew 27:3–4). Precisely because everything has been placed beyond the traitor's reach and control, the sense of the irreversibility of it all is overwhelming. There is nothing left to be done. Judas hangs himself, not as an act of atonement, it would seem, but rather because no work of atonement—from Judas—is possible.

Abandonment and betrayal

Scripture presents another figure, alongside Judas, who betrays his Lord. Peter is disloyal, not by handing Jesus over to the enemy, but simply by deserting him. Deserters as well as traitors are guilty of disloyalty. The traitor is disloyal to his country by selling it out; the deserter, by leaving it in the lurch. In betraying someone, I more or less deliberately hand him over to the enemy; in abandoning him, I simply leave him to the mercy of the elements. In the latter case, I may comfort myself with an optimistic reading of the circumstances into which I have thrown him, but it is not possible to deny the fact that among the elements, I am willing to risk the enemy.

Americans have a special feeling of uneasiness and guilt over the problem of desertion. The very act of settling in this country, of course, meant for the immigrants a separation from homeland and often from parents as well. This primordial act of desertion, moreover, has been repeated in the migrations of the modern middle class, whose children move from their homes to colleges, thence on to distant cities, where once again they move, on the average, every five years. Under these circumstances, ties with parents, brothers and sisters, and former friends are fitfully nourished with telephone calls or a flurry of cards at the Christmas season. The Bell Telephone Company and the Hallmark card industry grow rich on the conscience of Americans uneasy about their overextended personal loyalties. A failure in loyalty also makes itself felt in the modern American marriage. The husband who would not think to betray his wife through lust may be willing to abandon her to loneliness while he is absorbed in his work. Abandonment, desertion, and neglect, more often than deliberate betrayal, characterize the American sense of guilt over disloyalty.

At the same time, however, it must be admitted that the sin of desertion feeds on a certain truth. It is impossible to be everywhere at once. It is impossible to give one's self wholly to another even where one is. And when a man gives himself to others in a limited way, it is still necessary to conserve and preserve himself to make limited self-giving a possibility. To think otherwise on these matters is to entertain impossible assumptions about one's self. It is to regard one's self as absolutely indispensable to the life and well-being of others. The rejection of messianism is the truth on which the sin of desertion occasionally feeds. Peter acts on this truth. Sometimes it seems the most fitting thing to do— to abandon ship and save one's own skin.

The faithfulness of God through betrayal

At the outset of this essay it was pointed out that the church understands the event of Jesus Christ as the decisive disclosure of the faithfulness of God. Theologians have sought to describe this faithfulness by making reference to the divine constancy. In Jesus, God remains faithful to his promises, despite the fickleness and inconstancy of his creatures. He binds himself to man in a way in which a country would not bind itself to its citizens. He refuses to abandon man, even in the extremities of sin and death.

But the biblical account of the faithfulness of God contrasts strikingly with the analysis of the divine constancy that morality alone usually offers. Within the limits of morality, God's faithfulness usually refers to a certain intractability in the divine character. God's faithfulness and man's fickleness accordingly describe two separate lines—one straight, the other wavering— but two lines that never intersect. God's constancy traces a straight line above, while man's fickleness describes a wavering line below. Within these limits, no genuine intersection between God and man occurs. Sin is untouched from within. At best, men strive to imitate the unwavering steadfastness of God as it is disclosed in the Savior.

The surprising feature of the biblical account of the faithfulness of God is that God faithfully delivers men precisely through that event in which he delivers over his son into the hands of his enemies. God, in effect, is the chief of betrayers. Theologians have observed that the Greek word used in the New Testament for the verb "to betray" and the verb "to deliver" (in the sense of "redeem") can be the same. Salvation takes place only insofar as God enters into the unholy mechanism of betrayal itself, ripping it apart from within. God does not rescue men from the hands of sin and death at a distance. He does so in a form that is his own act of betrayal. He stands fast by men precisely in the act of "deserting" his son. He hands him over into the hands of sinners. He places him in the hands of a garrulous Peter, the silent Judas, the dedicated high priests, the ambiguous governor, and the fickle crowds. And, in turn, they hand him over from one to another until they deliver him at last to the grave. But the more rapidly they hand him on from one to another, the further they extend the faithfulness of God to the very end and limit of sin and death.

Christian fidelity

The Christian life calls for a trustworthiness and faithfulness in human relationships in response to the faithfulness of God. The problem of such fidelity is not solved by simple loyalty to persons at the expense of the claims of an institution or devotion to an institution to the exclusion of friendship. There is no way in which the Christian can escape the tensions between institutional standards and personal involvements. Simple loyalty to friends in any institutional setting produces bribery, injustice, and, ultimately, suspicion of betrayal. Simple devotion to an institution produces, on the other hand, a social structure that, humanly considered, is uninhabitable. The Christian life calls for a fidelity to persons that will not be intimidated by a social system, a sensitivity to objective standards that will not be corrupted by friendship. This much it requires without promise that all tension between friendship and structure, between friends and friends, or between friends and competitors will be removed.

So much the Christian shares with a more general understanding of the problems of fidelity. But there is a special act on the part of the Christian that distinguishes and determines his attempts to be faithful, both in friendship and in his professional setting. This is the act of intercessory prayer.

The biblical account of the faithfulness of God calls for a peculiar element of "betrayal" in the Christian life. This act of betrayal corresponds to God's deliverance of men through the betrayal of Jesus. Christian loyalty involves a "handing over" in response to the "handing over" of the Savior to men. The name for this strange ingredient in Christian loyalty is intercessory prayer.

If, in effecting their salvation, God handed over the Savior into the hands of men, in intercessory prayer, a man hands over other men into the hands of the Savior. This action mimics in its own way the mechanism of betrayal. In betrayal a man hands over his neighbor into the hands of the enemy. In intercessory prayer he hands over his friends, his competitors, and his enemies into the hands of God. In betrayal he loses control over the situation because the intentions of the enemy may differ from and outstrip his own. In intercessory prayer he loses control, because the purposes of God may exceed and contradict his own. This element of surrender cannot be overemphasized.

The intercessions of the heart are usually offered for those whom a man loves and over whom he exercises some control. Under these circumstances he is tempted to take himself too seriously. He is tempted to think of himself as the indispensable savior of those for whom he is responsible: his children, his students, his patients, and so forth. Improperly understood, intercessory prayer becomes little more than a covert extension of his own control. He merely implores God to be an extension of his own hands. He does not really give over the other to the Savior.

In intercessory prayer, properly understood, a man cannot merely move those for whom he prays from his right hand into his left. He must hand them over into the hands of God, both in the confidence that God will deal mercifully with his creatures and, because this is the case, that his dealings will not be restricted to the limits of the petitioner's imagination.

Such intercessory prayer has immediate moral consequences for the professional and personal life of a Christian and for a man's relationships to those for whom he prays, whether competitors or friends. When a man prays for his competitors he is henceforth forbidden the ploys of betrayal with them. He has already placed his competitors in hands beyond his reach. His act of intercession, therefore, places certain limits upon his behavior in a highly competitive and impersonal society. He cannot act as though he has free rein to hand his competitor over to disaster. He cannot act as though there are no positive responsibilities and standards of probity which are his in a harsh and aggressive environment.

By the same token, intercession places a certain constraint on friendship, but it is a limit of a different kind. When a man prays for his friends, he is forced to divest friendship—in either direction—of a messianic significance. An anxious control of others and an equally anxious dependence upon others is relinquished. To pray seriously for a friend is to surrender him into the hands of the Messiah. The way is opened up for a positive care and cherishing of others that is no longer a substitute for God. The moral implication of intercession is a certain carefree care for others in the Christian life. The pretensions of Atlas may be set aside. Loyalty has lost its sober face.

But this second moral consequence of intercession does not

directly touch the special American problem with which we began—the tension between social structure and social style. The American style of friendship, after all, is not of the idolatrous variety. A friendly immediacy with everyone, rather than an exclusive control or dependency upon one person, is the more usual American style. The religiously disturbing problem for this style is the intrusion of a social structure, hierarchical and impersonal, that forces the loss of friendly rapport. Human relations become oblique, indirect, partial, and specialized.

The Christian act of intercession does not call for a renunciation of the American social ideal. There is no proof that a new social style, marked by restraint, indirection, or hostility, for that matter, would be any closer to the Christian truth of things than the spontaneity, informality, openness, and directness of manner that has marked the American style at its best. However, the act of intercession does offer some relief from the compulsion that sometimes curses this style.

Of its very nature, intercessory prayer presupposes that another man's life is not exhausted by his relationship to the one who prays. There is a hard core of privacy in another's life, nothing less than the privacy of his relationship to God, which the man who prays, by the very act of praying, must accept. Because he runs up against the fact of this privacy in prayer, a man need not be disturbed by a social structure in which the life of another is not easily and fully available to him. He need not be disturbed by human relations which are no longer entirely open and direct. To be confronted by the mystery of another in one dimension permits one to cope with the removal of his person in another. Furthermore, intercession is based on the solid confidence that there is already a mediator between men. If there is indeed a mediator, not only between God and man but also between man and his friend, then the yearning for immediacy in both spheres is relieved of its terrible urgency. When we do not feel compelled to achieve immediacy, directness, and completeness in all human relations, then we are free to enjoy them when they unexpectedly come our way.

8 The Sin Against the Sexual Partner: LUST

There is no doubt that lust is the juiciest of the seven deadly sins, the sin with which the young, and sometimes the not-so-young, are most preoccupied. We may be made temporarily uneasy when lust is broken up into its various legal components: fornication, adultery, incest, seduction, rape, and unnatural vice, but few people today are hesitant to pursue their natural bent for the topic under its more fetching guise: sex. Denis de Rougemont once showed a comic sense of its attraction when he introduced a chapter on the "Devil and Sex" with words to this effect: To the adolescent among my readers who have turned to this chapter first. . . . And there one is, young or old, caught red-handed, eyes riveted, imagination stirred, ready for fresh rivulets of knowledge on that most pleasurable of the vices: lust.*

Lust takes its origin from a sexual passion in which the object of passion is not, finally, the sexual partner but rather the pleasure or services which the partner or the passion itself can provide. Historically, the church restricted its definition of lust primarily to the irresponsible pursuit of sexual enjoyment, although it recognized that the term had a secondary application to all excesses in the pursuit of pleasure. Thus Augustine, after the suggestion of Scripture, acknowledged the lust of the eyes as well as the lust of the flesh. Men can pursue the pleasures of knowledge just as relentlessly and destructively as the venereal pleasures of the body. The secondary applications of the term are important, but their validity does not argue against coming to

* Denis de Rougemont, *The Devil's Share* (New York: Pantheon Books, 1945).

grips, first and foremost, with its primary reference to relations between the sexes.

At first sight, it would appear that in our culture there are two great conflicting attitudes toward sex and love contending for the human heart. On the one hand, there is the officially sanctioned ethic of the West, sponsored originally by the church and protected in good part by the state, that holds a legalistic and suspicious, if not repressive, attitude toward sex, for it insists on marriage and monogamy, children, and a long list of responsibilities between two human beings, until death do them part. This tradition has been determined both in its Catholic and Protestant forms by a somewhat fearful attitude toward sex. Roman Catholicism has traditionally depreciated sexuality, even while holding to marriage as a sacrament, by insisting that the celibate life is more perfect, in principle, than the marital estate. Further, it devalued the erotic element in marriage by subordinating it to the task of procreation. Protestantism fared little better. After it emptied out the monasteries and the convents in many areas, it replaced them with the bourgeois institution of marriage, in which sexual love was rather strictly subordinated to the demands of the successful career.

Criticism of the historic Western position toward sex has taken two forms: sex-mysticism and sex-naturalism. The first is aesthetic, romantic, and religious in tone; the second, scientific and evangelically secular. The romantic tradition celebrates man's sexual passions with a religious fervor, finding them innately ennobling—whether in or out of marriage. In such a perspective, the classical tradition of the West seems hopelessly prosaic and rationalistic, reducing the mystery of love to everyday banalities. It casts a harsh, unaesthetic light on a darkly beautiful movement of the soul. The very use of the word "lust" by the historic religious tradition, with its ugly references to fornication and adultery, betrays its suspicious and somewhat pharisaical attitude toward a holy and sovereign force. The romantic usually admits, of course, that sexual passion is not all-sovereign. But far better —and more ennobling—that it encounter tragic conflict with the brutal claims of the world than that it be trivialized or repressed from within.

The naturalistic attack on the repressive sex ethics of the West is quite different from its romantic counterpart. Here it is not a question of darkness pitted against light, but rather a plea for more light; not a conflict between passion and prudence, but rather an appeal for more prudence. Man's sexual impulses, so the argument goes, are perfectly natural. They have neither the semidivine significance that they have for the romantic nor the semidemonic status that they had for many of the traditional Western moralists. Rather than being repressed, they need to be expressed as part of the natural bodily functions to which they belong. Only when erotic activity is arbitrarily restricted to marriage does the sexual impulse turn destructive, having lost its place among the resources at man's (and woman's) disposal for an integrated personal life. Admittedly, until recently there have been two serious arguments for the restriction of sexual intercourse to marriage partners—the possibilities of disease and pregnancy. But the developments of modern medicine have destroyed these arguments, and with them all grounds for an irrational fear of the sex act itself.

Although a similar line of reasoning has often been proposed in the back seats of cars, it is not without some validity. The Christian church ought not simply to defend the Western institution of marriage by standing blindly and menacingly alongside worried parents against the special sins of the young. Its judgments on the sin of lust must not fall into a Manichaean dualism, repelled by human sexuality. The ancient Hebrew circumcised the penis; he did not amputate it. Jesus forgave the adulterous woman; he did not stone her. The church's judgments on this sin, as on all others, must be directed toward life in covenant rather than toward death. Great care, then, must be taken in setting out the Christian context for its interpretation.

The Christian attitude toward sex fundamentally rejects the Manichaean belief that the body is intrinsically evil. As religious dualists who held to the radical opposition between the kingdom of spirit and the kingdom of flesh, the Manichaeans, quite logi-

cally, were opposed to sexual intercourse in general. Indeed, it
might be argued that they were especially opposed to sexual
intercourse in marriage as being particularly devoted to the
perpetuation of the human race on earth, thereby serving to
extend (through children) this present age and its evil confusion
of the two rival kingdoms. (Such an attitude should not be
totally unfamiliar. Although his myths may be somewhat different, many a modern pessimist has voiced a similar reluctance
about "bringing children into the world.")

The Christian church rejected this attitude, retaining the
memory of the wondrous fecundity of the patriarchs and kings of
Israel, children of promise and not the accidents of cosmic warfare. Torah urged Jews to cherish and discipline the body, not to
exterminate it. The Christian can do no less. His Savior came to
men in the full form of a man, soul and body. The community
receives him in earthly vessels of bread, wine, water, and oil. The
body is not the prison of the spirit but its natural home, the
temple of the Lord. The sin of the genitals can be a result only of
their misuse, not of their inherent evil.

But what, then, constitutes misuse, on man's part, of his sexuality? Any theoretical answer runs the risk of lapsing into a
pedantry comically inappropriate to the subject, a danger not
only for Christian moralists but also for those who are evangeli-
cal naturalists. Human sexuality is one of the realities in life
(death is another) that reminds a man that he does not have
himself and his career fully under control. Specifically it warns
the Christian against his spiritual pride—that is, against his confidence that he has his life fully theorized into a "Christian point
of view." Needless to say, this is a warning that the man of lust
(and the theoretical apologists for lust) also need to hear. George
Bernard Shaw put the comic quandary of the lustful very nicely
when he said that a man in pursuit of a woman may go after one
story but he always gets a second story along with it. The man
who praises the "natural, easy-come, easy-go, see-you-around"
view of sexuality knows little about the full gamut of human
emotions (jealousy, loneliness, vanity, suspicion, exuberance,
and so forth) that cluster around human sexuality, including his
own. He is an emotional prig who has to defend his priggishness

about women by calling them something other than women—
playmates or bunnies—in order to maintain toward them the
poise—and the pose—of a point of view.

Covenant love and the family

The Christian tradition, of course, directs and interprets full
sexual encounter in the context of marriage and the family. The
metaphysical basis for this high evaluation of marriage and the
family becomes dramatically clear if one considers once again
(but from a different angle) the special revulsion against community that one finds among the Manichaeans. Metaphysically,
the only acceptable model for human community for the
Manichaean is the model of the military organization. There is
no real possibility of community between entities that are both
distinct from one another and directed to each other. There is
only the possibility of organizing relatively homogenous entities
against an opposing force. Metaphysically, the Manichaean holds
to apartheid. There is either identity (as spirit is identical with
spirit) or there is opposition (as spirit and flesh are anathema to
one another), but there is no community between distinct entities. Perforce the Manichaean (and the military) must look
upon all contacts that are not guided by the needs of organized
opposition as enervating. Every military organization—monosexual as it is to its very core—has its problems with eros. The
more transient the contacts between the troops and the local
girls, the better off the organization from the point of view of
military discipline.

A metaphysical abhorrence not simply of sex but of marriage
lies at the heart of Manichaean thought. Thus its metaphors for
describing the relations between spirit and flesh are the familiar
ones of those who fear entanglements as a threat to military
apartheid. Spirit is "trapped" in the flesh, or, again, spirit and
flesh, in this present age, "commingle." Both metaphors are still
employed by those repelled by sex and marriage. Marriage is
considered a trap (instead of a covenant freely chosen) and the
sex act is abhorred as a messy, repugnantly intimate, and poten-

tially dangerous commingling. Much contemporary rhetoric on behalf of sexual promiscuity and freedom is also inspired by a monosexual abhorrence of "involvement."

The Christian approach to community is radically different from Manichaeism, because it is nourished by belief in the Trinity. For the Christian, there is a fundamental distinction in the Godhead itself between Father, Son, and Holy Spirit, and yet an indissoluble bond between them; a radical distinction between Creator and creature, and yet a covenant links them. Derivatively, there is a distinction between soul and body, but a self unites them; sexuality distinguishes man and woman, but the covenant of marriage binds them.

Far from minimizing those events in which a man promises himself to a woman and makes love to her, faith makes use of them to describe God's relation to his people. Specifically, according to the Prophets, God addresses his people as a lover and husband. " 'When I passed by you again and looked upon you, behold, you were at the age for love; and I spread my skirt over you, and covered your nakedness: yea, I plighted my troth to you and entered into a covenant with you, says the Lord God, and you became mine' " (Ezekiel 16:8). In continuance and consummation of this prophetic tradition, the Apostles referred to Christ as the bridegroom of the Church, and to the Christian himself as betrothed to Christ. These metaphors were not intended as poetical flights; indeed, they were used as a basis for apostolic instruction concerning human marriage. It would be the height of irony, therefore, for Christian judgment on lust to be controlled by the fears of the Manichaeans. Rather it must be guided by its own positive understanding of the possibility of covenant love between a man and a woman and the fruit of that love in progeny.

A natural law of sexuality?

In order to justify placing limits on the expression of sexuality, Christians have tried to show that their views on the question are not commitments to a metaphysics abstracted from the fundamental nature of the sex act itself. The argument that this limitation does not contradict nature takes two forms—one based on the procreative, and the other on the expressive (or revelatory) character of the sex act.

The first argument received prominence in traditional Roman Catholic theology. According to natural law theory, sex for man, as for all living beings, has its natural end in the reproduction of the species. This constitutes its proper fulfillment and therefore the law of its own nature. The reproduction of the species, however, is not properly achieved at the level of human existence unless the children enjoy extended care, nurture, and education. This work can be properly carried out only through the continuing co-operation of both parents. The only fitting context for the maturation of the young is the monogamous family. Therefore, indeterminate copulation between the sexes (although natural to some species) is ruled out for man as defying his own nature. Lust is simply that excessive love of venereal pleasure that prompts man to exceed or to contradict the proper end to which his sexual activity should be subordinate in the human family. Sacred Scripture has confirmed these judgments, based on natural law, in its positive commands concerning marriage ("be fruitful and multiply") and its negative judgments against fornication, adultery, onanism, sodomy, and all other sins that have their roots in lust.

Critics of this view have questioned whether the "nature" of sex can be derived from its procreative power alone without due regard for its meaning for the sexual partners themselves. The sex act has an expressive, as well as a procreative power; it is a revelatory event between two people. The question then is posed whether there is anything inherent in sexual intercourse that requires its restriction to marriage. Argument for such limitation can be developed in two ways.

The first argument depends upon the ultimate revelatory significance of the act. Love-making—just like a smile, a shrug, a smirk, or raised eyebrows—is a human gesture. Such gestures can be modified to a certain degree as to their import, but, on the whole, they have an intrinsic, and somewhat intransigent, meaning. In fact, human community depends upon a relative stability in their meaning. A shrug signifies resignation; a smirk, contempt; a smile, friendliness or amusement, and so forth. Such gestures, given and received, make human companionship possible. Correspondingly, when a discrepancy develops between the inner and the outer man, human community breaks down. When a smile says one thing, but the person behind the smile thinks and feels something else, gestures no longer establish and nourish community; quite the contrary, they destroy it. They are self-isolating acts.

This is the case in extremity for the act of sexual intercourse. It is the most intimate, complete, and unconditional unveiling of which two human beings are capable. As such, it is a gesture that is misleading and confusing whenever made in a context that is less than a total self-giving. Such giving, moreover, is more than an attitude of sincere feeling at a given moment. For better or for worse, human beings are distinguished from other creatures by their temporality. They cannot live in the present alone. The whole self cannot be given—however fervent the gesture—if the future is reserved.

From this perspective, then, lust is sexual activity whose ultimate expressive power is violated for the sake of pleasure in the moment. The satisfaction of one's own bodily desires supersedes the power of the act to reveal love and to receive love revealed. The gesture of love is made, but it conceals a self-love by which its movements are ultimately controlled.

The question occurs, of course, whether a couple cannot hedge against the ultimate revelatory import of the gesture by candid and mutual acknowledgement that the act does not have this kind of significance for them. Certainly, such honesty is better than dishonesty, but the device is flawed by a certain pedantry. It is difficult to make a gesture—whether it is a handshake or a smile—and then launch into a discourse pointing out to the recipient that the gesture does not carry its ordinary meaning. No one should have to take on such a heavy pedagogical burden, preceding or following the act of sexual intercourse. Only an emotional prig could relish it, by systematically ignoring the awkwardness, the groping, the reticence, and the importuning that characterize the act as a human unveiling. When sexual intercourse is theoretically reduced to the discharge of sexual energies for the sake of personal adjustment and pleasure, its revelatory import is ignored.

This argument for the limitation of sexual intercourse to marriage unfortunately lapses into sentimentalism whenever it regards the act as an ultimate breakthrough between human beings. (In the older collegiate jargon, it was called a "Meaningful Experience," more recently, an I-Thou encounter.) Mystics to the contrary, however, the earth does not tremble, or the mountains fall, with the experience of sexual ecstasy. No act of love-making is the equivalent of Exodus, Mt. Sinai, or the Resurrection of Christit:* a unique, once-and-for-all event so consummate in character as never to need repeating. Quite the contrary, the act of sexual intercourse is an eminently repeatable event, enriched in renewal under the varied conditions that make up married life. Thus a second line of argument needs to be developed on behalf of marriage as the normative context for love-making. It is not the sovereign triumph of a single act of love but rather its triumph, edged with incompleteness, that requires a covenant for its full context. Love calls for the continuance of love. Its success is also a poignant defeat that urges success once again. This second argument depends less on the ultimate expressive power of the act than upon its power to nourish love—so long as its context is continuing love.

In an essay on the question of sexual relations outside of marriage, Professor Paul Ramsey has managed to value sexual partnership in such a way as to avoid the sentimentality of the sex-mystics. At the same time he surmounts the stalemate between some Catholics and Protestants on the question as to whether procreation or partnership is the primary end of marriage by insisting on them both together in unity.

> An act of sexual intercourse is an act of love. It is also an act of procreation. Whether or not an existing relation between the man and woman is actually nourished and strengthened

---

* D. H. Lawrence strained for the comparison in *Lady Chatterly's Lover* when he parodied the Psalm: "Let the king of glory enter in."

by this sexual intercourse, the act itself is an act of love with this power. Whether or not a child is engendered, the act is in itself procreative. This means that sexual intercourse tends of its own nature toward the expression and strengthening of love and toward the engendering of children. . . . These are among the chief goods of marriage.*

By stating that the act tends toward the "expression" of love, Professor Ramsey does justice to its revelatory power, but by adding the phrase, "and strengthening of love," he implies that no given act need be valued beyond its human power to nourish repeatedly.

When all has been said and done, however, it is doubtful whether interpretation of the sex act leads unambiguously to the monogamous family. The proponents of the new morality have a point when they eschew its procreative and revelatory powers and settle for its obvious pleasures. After all, sex is a source of self-satisfaction, whatever its powers of self-communication may be. (Not that the desire for pleasure contradicts the expression and nurture of love. Indeed, love can be nourished even when the only immediate intent of the act is mutual satisfaction in the body of another.) But the impulse to pleasure in the sex act is, to say the least, not wholly domesticated. Although it may serve— and serve exuberantly—the ends of love and paternity, it is never simply coincident and subordinate to them.

It would seem, therefore, that prior commitments of the Christian, rather than an independent analysis of the sex act itself, prompt him to subordinate the varied and vagrant impulses that inform his sexuality to the ends of covenant love and the family. The value of such independent analysis is not that it produces a natural law of sexuality, but that it makes clear that Christian morality, unlike Manichaeism, does not exult in the unnatural. There are, in truth, tendencies in the act to the expression of love, fleshly pleasure, and the begetting of children. The lively

* Paul Ramsey, "A Christian Approach to the Question of Sexual Relations Outside of Marriage," *The Journal of Religion*, XLV, No. 2 (April 1965), p. 100.

and somewhat discordant relations of these three tendencies simply remind us of the element of spiritual pendantry in presenting a "position" on the subject, a comic posture no less evident today in missionaries for sexual freedom than in evangelists for the Victorian household.

Lust with the heterosexual partner

The medieval tradition includes fornication, adultery, rape, and sodomy among the various types of lust. The difficulty with this classification is that lust is primarily a specific motive for sexual action rather than an external act. Lust has been defined as a sexual passion in which the object of passion is not, finally, the sexual partner but rather the pleasures or services which the partner or the passion itself can provide. In lust, the desire for sexual self-satisfaction takes precedence over the claims of covenant love and progeny. Not all instances of fornication, adultery, and homosexuality, however, although they may be objectionable on other grounds, are motivated by lust. Their leading motives may be self-pity, revenge, pity, avarice, and so forth, to which the motive of lust may be quite subordinate.

The classification offered here is threefold: lust with the heterosexual partner, lust with the homosexual partner, and lust without a sexual partner. The repetition of the term lust in each case serves as a reminder that we are dealing with a specific motive for irresponsibility: the desire for sexual gratification. While exploring this irresponsibility in three spheres, we will be able to remind ourselves of the complexity of the motives that operate in those external acts normally subsumed under the topic of lust.

a. FORNICATION Legally considered, the term covers a rather considerable range of premarital sexual activity. For the high school and collegiate adolescent, premarital intercourse is but the goal line that lends interest to the petting game. In this case, the final act may be an expression of lust but hardly less so than the game itself, by virtue of which a woman has already been marked out like a football field. For the mature man and woman, sexual intercourse is one of the ingredients of an affair in which the chief uncertainty becomes simply how long and under what terms the affair will last. In such an affair, there may be more directness and honesty than the adolescent finds himself capable of, but a certain melancholy also hangs over it all. Temporary arrangements are not the same thing as a permanent vow. Giving presents is not the same thing as giving one's self. Strict honesty about the reservations with which the sexual act is committed is not quite the same thing as the act itself performed as a truthful testament of love.

There is, still further, the young man who is bound to a girl by a certain affection and who moves imperceptibly and unreflectively from intercourse into commitments and from commitments into marriage, or, alternatively, who gets engaged rather carelessly for the purpose of sexual freedom and suddenly finds himself tidily bound in marriage. Lust in these cases is a subordinate problem. Sexual intercourse occurs, but it represents a failure rather than a triumph of male passion. The whole event transpires in the course of a fatal passivity; the young man has not yet awakened from the drowsiness of adolescence and come into the full possession of his powers as a responsible adult. Lust has led him into a problem which he solves by compounding it. He takes the step society accepts as a sign of formal responsibility, but he himself remains irresponsible. Drifting into the marriage he expects of himself because he sleeps with the girl, he defers the problems of becoming a decisive man to a later, and tragically more expensive, date.

Finally there is the couple, committed to one another without reserve, except that they have not yet gone through the civil or ecclesiastical rites. Legally considered, they also are fornicators, but, as Professor Ramsey has argued in the article cited earlier, their sexual relations are, in fact, marital rather than premarital from the point of view of the Christian faith.

The variety of conditions and motives that attend the act as it is legally defined makes it impossible to subsume fornication entirely under the subject of lust.

b. ADULTERY   Some people flatter themselves that promiscuity is evidence of a superabundance of sexual passion. No doubt, this can be the case. There are persons who are ready to play havoc with covenants, however solemnly undertaken, for the sake of sexual pleasure. There are others who believe that their sex life is but an extension of childhood play, a world in which castles can be built and torn down according to inexhaustible impulse, without a shadow of regret. But a variety of other motives are usually present in the extramarital affair—self-pity, anger, curiosity, sympathy, boredom, vanity, loneliness, and self-contempt. It would take a novelist to reconstruct the complexity of motive in a given case. Interpreters as divergent as Denis de Rougemont, T. S. Eliot, and Paddy Chayefsky have recognized that a sexual crisis may be prominent in adultery but not necessarily the crisis of sexual excess. The quest for a success outside of marriage may be prompted by one's inability to be fervent in marriage. Unable to love satisfactorily the woman who occupies his bed, a man may seek to prove his potency with others. In such cases sexual promiscuity gives evidence of a failure rather than a triumph in sexual passion.

c. LUST IN MARRIAGE   The institution of marriage itself has been so sentimentalized in the United States as to cause persons to overlook the fact that marriage itself does not magically solve the problem of lustful behavior. Lust in marriage is more subtle than dramatic instances of masochistic, sadistic, and other deviant patterns of behavior. More important is a certain routine mechanization of sex that occurs precisely when the erotic element in marriage has disappeared. Ironically, lust looms largest as a problem when a marriage has become organized around extrasexual aims; life is absorbed elsewhere and the sexual element in marriage is reduced to the services rendered by the mechanics of the act. When a businessman has geared his life rigidly to achievement in his job (his psychic and somatic tensions increasing accordingly) and when his wife similarly orients herself to the manic demands and prestige of his position, precisely, then, sexuality no longer informs the whole persons. The act of intercourse merely provides certain calculated consequences for the hard-pressed couple by way of routine pleasure and sleep.

The way is prepared for this instrumentalization of sex in marriage in the preceding patterns of American dating. Each becomes proficient in a set of techniques, and uses the other for the sake of a certain victory—the man seeking a sexual victory and the girl a social victory. After marriage, the aim of the girl remains much the same; the aim of the man changes to become more nearly hers. Thus both, now married, continue to use their marriage, indeed exhaust their marriage, in the pursuit of a social victory from which they may never relax because the goal line recedes in the distance, no matter how hard they run. In this frigid atmosphere lust becomes the only residue of sexuality.

Lust with the homosexual partner

There is no doubt that historic Christianity considers the heterosexual partnership as normative in human affairs. Covenant partnership between distinctive beings and the fruit of that partnership in children are not only the chief goods of marriage but of sexuality itself.

Scripture explicitly interprets homosexuality as an abnormality that contravenes the basic modes of fellowship between man and woman and man and man. According to St. Paul, homosexuality is both sinful and unnatural: "For this reason God gave them up to dishonorable passions. Their women exchanged natural relations for unnatural, and the men likewise gave up natural relations with women and were consumed with passion for one another, men committing shameless acts with men and receiving in their own persons the due penalty for their error" (Romans 1:26–27).

Modern liberal opinion has tended to criticize this scriptural judgment against homosexuality. It interprets homosexuality as a natural disposition—variant though it may be—rather than as a moral error. It admits that there may be pathological cases of homosexuality, but it reminds us that part of the blame for such tragedies must be assigned to the heterosexual majority whose harsh, unaccepting, and oftentimes sadistic attitudes place an insupportable burden on homosexuals seeking to adjust to their condition.

Recent studies have complicated the picture. While taking account of the physico-psychological factors in homosexuality, they question whether the homosexual himself has not tended to exaggerate the importance of natural factors as an explanation for his sexual behavior. Presumably he perpetuates the myth that his attitude is fatefully determined because it relieves him of personal responsibility, furnishing him with a ready excuse for not undertaking treatment. Additionally, his myth is useful to him both in courtship ("we're fated") and in defense against the self-righteous mockery of a heterosexual world.

The debate apparently has not been concluded. This fact urges caution in Christian statement, but it does not mean that Christian comment waits entirely upon its outcome. Certain things can be said both about the relationship of the church to the homosexual and about the relationship of the Christian homosexual to the discipline of his faith.

First, the church cannot afford simply to side with the avenging angels of the heterosexual world against the homosexual—even if it should be the case that the homosexual has greater responsibility for his predilections than he is inclined to admit. Christian love does not wait upon proof of sinlessness in coming to heterosexuals; it can be no less responsive to homosexuals.* Indeed, particularly if homosexuality is a result of personal responsibility and choice, the Christian community cannot afford to reproach the homosexual with harsh words of judgment abstracted from its positive message of grace and calling. It is a betrayal of her task for the church to obscure that very grace

---

* It should be noted that St. Paul's comments on homosexuality are made in the context of a passage on the *various* sins. It concludes: "Therefore you have no excuse, O man, whoever you are, when you judge another; for in passing judgment upon him you condemn yourself, because you, the judge, are doing the very same things" (Romans 2:1).

which the homosexual may desire and need in making his most responsible choices. It is also a betrayal for a middle-class church, oversentimental about the institution of marriage, to ignore the vocation of many homosexuals—and heterosexuals as well—to the positive calling of the celibate life. However, the church cannot atone for past sins of self-righteousness by refusing to deal with the moral issues which the homosexual himself has to face. How effective is the church's ministry of love if it is eaten away by the fear that it cannot care for someone unless it is able to gloss over his real difficulties? Reflection is required then on the second issue of the homosexual's relation to the discipline of the Christian faith.

It must first be said that scriptural judgments on homosexuality ought not to be cast aside lightly. Just as the Christian, in respect for Jesus' teachings, would try to exhaust all available means to save his troubled marriage before determining on divorce, the Christian who finds himself susceptible to homosexual passion would exhaust all available means to save his troubled celibate life before determining on a different course. This does not mean that the injunctions of the celibate Paul are the only and final word to be said on the subject of homosexuality. But it does mean that from extrascriptural studies one should seek knowledge on the subject, rather than a rationalization of one's own desires. Second, even if it is recognized that the homosexual may not be able to control his general disposition toward men, it should not be assumed that he is unable to exercise discretion over the forms that his love takes. Love is not an indeterminate, fateful force, but an involvement with a concrete, specific human being. This is what distinguishes it from lust. No one can love a specific person without raising fundamental questions as to who he is and what his final destiny might be. Lucid answers to these questions in specific cases may demand from the homosexual that his love take the form of restraint.

Finally, it may be somewhat misleading—and not particularly helpful to the homosexual—to discuss the difficulties he faces in the framework of lust. Such discussion gives too much notice to his difficulty as a sexual problem, and too little attention to its satellite temptations. Perhaps it would be more useful to understand his difficulties as they distribute themselves across the broad spectrum of human temptation, while recognizing the special form that each problem takes for him.

For example, pride tempts the homosexual in the manner in which it usually tempts a member of a minority group. When men find themselves treated as social outcasts, excommunicated by the smiles (in this case) of the heterosexual majority, they are tempted to retaliate by asserting their inherent cultural superiority to their philistine persecutors. This pride may also figure in the homosexual's peculiar turn of taste for the precious and the bizarre, a pride not unlike that of the ancient Gnostics, whose sense of superiority depended upon their cultivation of the exotic.

Avarice, too, can be a difficulty for the homosexual—in the peculiar way in which we have extended the scope of the term to include not only the love of possessions but also the adoption of a possessive and managerial relation to others. Homosexuality, on occasion, may not corrupt ordinary friendship so much by lust as by avarice. The older, more experienced, and powerful individual in a pair of men may substitute for the reciprocal freedom of friendship the more subtle, involuted patterns of pleasure that go with systems of sponsorship, manipulation, and control.

Finally, where homosexuality is concentrated in certain businesses and professions, there is the temptation to practice that injustice (which the heterosexual community has already perfected) of making business decisions on the basis of private sexual interests and prejudices.

The silence of Christian moralists on these and other issues which the homosexual faces is irresponsible. There is no reason why the homosexual, any more than any other man, should have to assume that the spirit's cries for help will go unheard.

Lust without a sexual partner

If love is an absorbing involvement in another person and if lust is a failure in that involvement in favor of the pleasure or services which the person provides, then the final stage of lust is that occluded state in which the partner is no longer necessary as the dispenser of sexual pleasure. In autoerotic activity, in the cult of romantic love, and in voyeurism and pornography, the partner is dispensed with.

Sexual phenomena of this kind are ambivalent. On the one hand, they are the dead end of sexuality; a man's capacity to celebrate his own body in the body of another is stalled in futility. On the other hand, these phenomena are experienced most acutely by those in the nascent stages of sexuality, precisely those who are on their way toward the possibilities of sexual partnership. It would be a grievous error, then, to deal with the subject in such a way as to produce guilt feelings over, and revulsion for, sexuality as such. The morbid preoccupations of adolescent sexuality would only be needlessly prolonged. And yet, precisely before sexuality succeeds in reaching the partner, what it means to fail in reaching partnership may be sensitively revealed. Even though transient, these phenomena give a glimpse into sexuality at a dead end. It is enough to consider the cult of romantic love and voyeurism.

a. The Cult of Romantic Experience If love is an absorbing involvement with another person, then romantic love—in which the center of attention is ultimately not another person but rather the emotions that he or she inspires—is actually deficient in sexual passion. Falling in love with Love is not love but rather a blurred experience of lust. There are differences between the lustful man, narrowly defined, and the romantic. The lustful man is usually a hedonist (or a pervert who seeks his pleasure in pain); the romantic is an idealist whose treasured experiences transcend the simple crudities of pleasure-calculus. The lustful man measures his own well-being in terms of the success or failure of his adventures in sex. The romantic, on the other hand, has a distinct bias toward the otherworldly, the exalted, and the tragic. He thrives just as much on the failure of sexual union as on its success. Indeed, his experience is enhanced and intensified by the conflict between yearning and deprivation, whether that deprivation is caused by the villainies of objective circumstance or the cruelties of unrequited love. These differences between the lustful and the romantic, with respect to the tones of experience to which they are drawn, cannot obscure the similarity of their plight. Both are finally given to occlusion and withdrawal, insofar as they treat the other person as an instrument or occasion for the self's own erotic adventures.

b. Voyeurism The term "voyeur" applies narrowly to the solitary deviate who is either too terrified to approach a woman directly, and who, therefore, seeks what will be for him a more intense experience—peeping through a transom. More broadly applied, the term refers to the denizens of the peep shows, who are either too young and shy to handle a woman, too respectably married to get involved with one, or too old and unattractive to win one. But there is a sense in which the term can be more broadly applied, indeed, so as to become coextensive with the entire culture in which we live. For we live in an age in which voyeurism is no longer the side line of the solitary deviate but rather a national pastime, fully institutionalized and naturalized in the mass media.

Some interpreters have taken our fascination with exhibited sex as a sign of our sensual vitality, the exuberance of a people liberated from the Victorian corset. They feel that we are at last living in an age in which people can publicly savor and enjoy God's good green gift of sexuality. The assumptions of this view are questionable, and the plight of the solitary voyeur is symptomatic. People do not become obsessed with sex-on-view because of the strength but because of the weakness of their passions. When the direct presence of another person no longer excites, then voyeurism can become a national pastime. More than one couple has made late TV a habit because they do not know how to go to bed.

Voyeurism is more than a sign of the weakness of passion, however; it is also a sly avoidance of personal responsibility. The observer, after all, in sex (as well as in politics and entertainment) is doing nothing. He is only standing and watching. With charming and syncopated candor, the Broadway musical *Most Happy Fella* describes the advantages that accrue to the voyeur "standing on the corner watching all the girls go by"; everything is transposed to the order of the imagination, and therefore he is relieved of all responsibility.

Somewhat less savory are the tactics of the indoor voyeur at the peep show. In this case what he watches is so visibly vulgar that he does not even want to be identified as a watcher. Indeed he would be greatly embarassed if overtures were made that would single him out of the audience. He wishes to remain inconspicuous. With head ducked, he is Mr. No-name. He prefers simply to be left alone to enjoy the pleasures of his own stimulated imagination.

The voyeur completes his retreat from contact with others through the services of pornographic literature. Here the transposition of sex from the actual world to the order of the imagination is complete. The chief danger of pornographic literature is not that it inspires its reader (the adolescent, the traveler, the soldier, the loner) to go out and do likewise (although it is true that brothels make use of pictures to stimulate performance) but that this literature substitutes an intense imaginative experience for actual contact with another human being. Sexuality, in other words, becomes abstract; it is detached from personal loyalty and love. Pornography performs the indubitable service of clotting the arteries with pleasure while cutting out the heart and the self. Not only the sexual partner but also the self has vanished. This is the dead end of lust, its pointless extremity in gratification alone.

The Strategy
and Atmosphere of Sin

9 The Utility Sin:
DECEIT

In the medieval tradition the various sins are distinguished by the
end that a man pursues in each case—lust, money, public reputation, and so forth. Deceit, however, is distinct from the other sins
in that it pursues no particular end but rather serves whatever
end is pursued. Deceit is the strategy of sin rather than the goal of
the campaign. Lying is the utility sin, if you will, whose aim it is
to serve the others. Types of lies can be classified according to the
sin, or sins, pursued in each case.

Lying in the service of pride is boasting (*jactantia*). Boasting
is the propaganda of pride. *Jactare* means literally "to throw";
to boast is man's attempt to boost himself above his fellow
creatures through words. It takes, however, a rather considerable
effort because of the dead weight of the reality. Only in pathological lying does this weight disappear, when the self becomes
as light as a feather and the boaster can say anything about
himself without deterrent.

Lying can also serve the opposite interests of boredom, gluttony, and dejection. Here the primary movement of man is
downward, away from God; he seeks to deflate his world or belit-
tle himself in order to excuse his torpor, his appetite, or his

melancholy. Professional self-belittlement is no closer to the truth than compulsive self-inflation. In both cases the fundamental distortion is that the self has made itself the center of the universe.

Lying in the service of malice and envy is slander. It means bearing false witness against one's neighbor. But less obviously, it can mean telling the truth about one's neighbor—but a shrewdly factual truth which, by virtue of its timing, its audience, and its inflection, is most designed to hurt. There is a kind of lying involved in telling such truths, even when formally considered they are beyond reproach. In envy and malice we may tell the truth about our neighbor, but is it the truth that we have served in its telling? There is such a thing as a little black truth.

Lying in the service of lust is insincerity; sweet lies are told, and accepted, for the sake of the sin. Lying in the service of faintheartedness may mean the exaggeration of evils confronting one's self or, conversely, their systematic avoidance through circumlocution. We refuse to name realities too unbearable to face, like death. Men do not die, they pass away; and before their death most men avoid the truth of their condition with the help of substitute diagnoses. Similarly, lying in the service of neglect often means the resort to euphemisms. The poor become the "underprivileged" so as to preserve their dignity, to be sure, but also their invisibility.

The attempt to deceive God

The purpose of lying or deceit in the service of sin is to fool one of three persons: God, the neighbor, or the self. The very term "fool," of course, betrays an element of contempt that is involved in deceit. Even while showing contempt, however, deceit involuntarily admits the dignity of the person deceived as a rational and moral being. Often we unwittingly honor those whom we seek to deceive, when we half-fear what their action would be if they knew the truth.

To deceive God is an impossibility because he is omniscient. Nevertheless, religious men seek to hide from him in two ways:

by not going to church or by going to church. By not going to church they hope to avoid having to see him just now; by going to church, they may hope to fool him about what they are doing elsewhere. But either way, hiding from him is doomed to failure. He knows us better than we know ourselves. If God is omniscient, then sin can never be accomplished out of his sight. The Prophets recognized this fact when they made the harsh comparison of Israel in her sinning with an animal copulating in public.

God's omniscience, however, is not simply that of an electronically equipped detective who knows everything. It is based scripturally on his personal confrontation with men in judgment and grace. God does not know sin because he is the police sergeant in charge of the files, but because he has made himself a part of the dossier. "For we have not a high priest who is unable to sympathize with our weaknesses, but one who in every respect has been tempted as we are, yet without sinning" (Hebrews 4:15).

If it is impossible to deceive God in sin, then the attempts to do so must really be essays in self-deceit and in deception of one's neighbor. This is indeed the way in which the common tradition has understood the problem under the rubric of hypocrisy—the special sin of the religious man. The hypocrite pretends to be on candid terms with God in order to impress himself and his neighbor.

Self-deceit

In each sin a man defies both God and his own place in the world. We have tried to emphasize this fact by resort to the phrase "instead of." *Instead of* living *in* the world, the idolatrous man and the fainthearted man fall under the spell of the world. *Instead of* living *with* their neighbors, the envious, the malicious, the neglectful, the traitorous, and the lustful defiantly choose to mistreat their neighbors.

The primary function of self-deceit is to obscure this element of defiance. This is done by reshaping the world and God in advance, so that they conform to the sinner's intentions. In this

way sin appears to reflect reality as it is rather than to promote
its contradiction.* Every sinner is his own landscape artist and
portrait painter, re-creating the countryside and peopling it according to his own imagination. Thus we can speak of the "world
of avarice," the "world of envy," the "world of betrayal," the
"world of lust," and so forth. There is no reason to represent
these worlds in detail in the course of this essay, because this has
been one of the intentions of the book as a whole. The review of
each in cameo will suffice.

The idolatrous man does not believe that he has imposed his
idol on the world but that the world organizes itself around the
idol. The fainthearted do not recognize that they have partly
conjured the evils before which they recoil; they are convinced
that catastrophe constantly threatens. The envious do not realize
that they have actively sought out the rich in contrast to whom
they may feel outrageously poor; they see the universe as flaunt-
ing this injustice in their faces. It is the same with the rest of the
sins. For those in the throes of hatred, the world seems a theater
in which the enemy constantly occupies center stage; and for the
neglectful, the needy seems to disappear from view because of a
harmless tendency to near- or far-sightedness. So also, traitors, the
lustful, and deceivers may argue the necessity, or the naturalness,
of their betrayals and lies. The proud man assumes that he gives
the self its own just due—not that he is glorifying it arbitrarily.
And the bored man cannot admit that he has committed spiritual suicide; the world around him has simply died.

Further, in self-deceit, a man helps to *create* the very world he
pictures. Thus he confirms the lies he tells himself. The irony is
that certain false theories, as they are lived out, tend to *create*
facts in their support. The rationalizations of sin are demiurgic:
the hostile man not only thinks he has enemies; his hostility
tends to produce them. The anxious man's very indecisiveness
further infects his environment with uncertainty.

Self-deception, however, never wins a total victory. A man is

* "But if you are harboring bitter jealousy and selfish ambition in your
hearts, consider whether your claims are not false, and a defiance of the
truth" (James 3:14). [New English Bible translation.]

both deceived and straining to be deceived. This tension distinguishes self-deception from pathological delusion and from the hallucinations of the demented. The emotionally deranged man holds to a view of the world foreign to the real world, and, since nothing is capable of contradicting his delusion, he is totally fixed within it. The "bondage" of man to sin, however, is not a bondage to a particular sin in the sense that a man is so deluded by its world outlook that he no longer has to strain to maintain it. At some level of his being, the self-deceived man is capable of recognizing the element of fabrication in his deception. Were it not so, his sin would no longer be sin, but pathological compulsion.

Deception of the neighbor

Lying about the neighbor (slander) is different from deceiving the same neighbor directly (hypocrisy, insincerity, and so forth); but the effectiveness of a slanderous lie about one neighbor depends upon deceiving yet another.

Lying to the neighbor is more than a deliberate doctoring of the facts. It distorts the facts, but it also distorts the speaker. The speaker gives the impression of having a commitment to the listener, but underneath he sustains another that prompts his lie. A fatal discrepancy develops therefore between the inner and the outer man, the will and the words, the heart and the face. Lying always involves putting a different face not only on things but on one's self as well. In Dante's *Inferno,* the falsifiers and the hypocrites suffer appropriately from diseases of the skin. Lying is moral eczema. Of falsifiers, Dante writes:

> I saw two sitting propped against each other as pan is propped on pan to warm, spotted from head to foot with scabs; and I never saw curry-comb plied by a stable-boy . . . as each plied on himself continually the bite of his nails for the great fury of the itch that has no other relief. . . . *

* Dante's *Inferno,* trans. John D. Sinclair (New York: Oxford University Press, 1961), Canto XXIX, ll. 73–81, p. 363.

Seen in this light, deceit is a more serious vice than the occasional, deliberate misrepresentation of facts. Formal lying about objective facts may be episodic, but deceit, in the sense of a discrepancy between the inner and the outer man, can become a way of life. Fatal differences develop between the "thing in itself" and the face it shows to the world—between the contents and the packaging. The public image becomes more important than the private reality, the book jacket more important than the actual text. The blare of press-agentry distracts from the deeper movements of the spirit; a public sheen hides the soul from view. There is something deceptive, eerie, and disappointing about a cheerfulness that wards off intimacy, a cataract of energy that does not allow for a revealing pause, or an unfailing friendliness that fails in friendship. Deceit of the neighbor abuses a man's capacity to reveal himself to his neighbor—to be with his neighbor in truth.

The Gospel of John calls the devil the "father of all lies" (John 8:44). It is from the devil that we may learn something about the deceit of the neighbor in its extremity. *

Apart from his general attractiveness to all men, the devil has a peculiar appeal for the actor. No performer turns down a chance to play the part of the devil because the role lets him play at least a dozen other roles. The Tempter himself is a consummate actor.

An actor, of course, is not a liar; the list of *Dramatis Personae* keeps us informed as to his true identity; but the devil is an actor without any identity whatsoever. This is what makes him the chief of all liars. He is able to play a variety of roles because he is not an identifiable being alongside of other beings. There is nothing in him that limits him to playing certain parts. Metaphysically considered, the devil is nothing. Precisely because he is nothing, he can pretend to be anything. Because he is nowhere, he can seem everywhere. Nothing restrains him—certainly not a

* Those familiar with Søren Kierkegaard's *The Concept of Dread,* trans. Walter Lowrie (Princeton: Princeton University Press, 1946), and Denis de Rougemont's *The Devil's Share* (New York: Pantheon Books, 1945), will recognize their influence on the following analysis of the demonic.

specific character of his own—from promising what he pleases. He is wholly unaccountable, both to himself and his victim, and that is why he is also considered in Scripture a relentless accuser (Revelation 12:10). The very same void that is at the ground of his lies is at the basis of his accusations. He cannot be relied upon. He may promise everything, but there is no one there in faith to keep promises. And so the moment he has a man, he is the first to abandon him. He is the first to take delight in the disappointment of the gulled.

The devil is the chief of liars and wholly unreliable because there is an absolute discrepancy between within and without. Outside he is one thing after another; inside he is nothing. Man is a liar, but not the chief of liars, because there is a relative discrepancy between within and without, between feeling and gesture. Outside he is one thing; inside he may be another. There remains now the task of analyzing the assertion of faith that God is the truth.

Promise and judgment

The sense in which God is the truth has been presupposed throughout this analysis of deceit: it means straightforwardly that God is faithful in his Word. There is no discrepancy between what God is in himself and what he is in his relevation of himself. He makes promises and he is faithful to his promises. Whereas the word of the devil stands only for the instant, and the word of man only for the time being, God's Word stands forever: ". . . It is because the Lord loves you, and is keeping the oath which he swore to your fathers, that the Lord has brought you out with a mighty hand, and redeemed you from the house of bondage, from the hand of Pharaoh king of Egypt. Know therefore that the Lord your God is God, the faithful God who keeps covenant and steadfast love. . . ." (Deuteronomy 7:8-9)

God is also faithful in his word of judgment. In fact, God's faithfulness in promise is, at the same time, a judgment. He exposes man in the unreliability of his own word—but never in the arbitrary fashion of demonic accusation.

Judgment is a pronouncement that is consistent with a certain criterion or standard. It is a Word from God perfectly consistent with his previous word. The devil's accusation is a stream of malice, consistent with no previous word from his mouth. His accusation is possible only in the void of a lie. He goes back on his words of enticement with a string of accusations which show that his previous word meant nothing. Wholly a void, he is the wildest of liars and the worst of accusers.

The event in which the Christian recognizes the fulfillment of God's word of promise and judgment is Jesus Christ. This is the reason Scripture asserts "the truth is in Jesus" (Ephesians 4:21), or again, "I am the way, and the truth, and the life" (John 14:6). There are three possible meanings that might be assigned to the proposition that Jesus is the truth, none of which may be omitted in a full interpretation of the statement.

First, Jesus might be true in the sense that he spoke *truly* about man and God. Jesus did not distort in his teaching "the way things are both in regard to God and in regard to man." For the Christian, Jesus is the truth in this first sense that his teachings are true.

Second, he might be true in the sense that there is no discrepancy in him between the inner and the outer man. He did not offer a religious format designed to impress the world. He lived and spoke with all the candor of Gethsemane: "My Father, if it be possible, let this cup pass from me; nevertheless not as I will but as thou wilt." Not only then is his word true, he is true to his word. There is no flamboyant word, no religious rigging that would suggest a fatal discrepancy between his gesture and the soul that lies behind it.

But, for the Christian, there is a third and decisive sense to the proposition that Jesus is the truth: he is God's word, deed, or gesture, addressed to men. He is more than a man who points to God and more than a man who, when he points to God, is truly himself. He is a man who is God's own word to man, that is, a word to man in which God is truly himself.

Put another way, when the early church affirmed that he is

true God from true God and true light from true light, the
community affirmed that in Christ, the church really meets God
and *not* God's format. If God in himself were one thing, and
God in this event momentarily and casually something different,
then faith in Christ would be nonsense. It would be foolish to
cling to a surface brilliance of the divine, while behind in the
darkness lurks an altogether different sort of power.

The truth is in Jesus in the sense that he is the gesture of God
toward man, the disclosure of divine forgiveness, the unleashing
of divine power to which men can really hold because God does
not reserve himself behind, above, or beyond this event as someone else. This is at issue in the confrontation reported by John:

> Philip said to him, "Lord, show us the Father, and we shall
> be satisfied." Jesus said to him, "Have I been with you so long,
> and yet you do not know me, Philip? He who has seen me has
> seen the Father; how can you say, 'Show us the Father?' Do you
> not believe that I am in the Father and the Father in me? The
> words that I say to you I do not speak on my own authority;
> but the Father who dwells in me does his works."
>
> John 14:8–10

The man of truth

The key passage in Deuteronomy cited earlier in this chapter
associates God's truthfulness with his love. God is truthful first
and foremost in keeping faith with his promises of mercy to men:
" '. . . it is because the Lord loves you, and is keeping the oath
which he swore to your fathers. . . .' " (Deuteronomy 7:8) Calvin
also observed the connection between love and truth in the
Psalms: ". . . the two things, mercy and truth, are uniformly con-
joined in the Psalms as having a mutual connection with each
other. For it were no avail to us to know that God is true, did he
not in mercy allure us to himself. . . ."[*] This connection between
truth and love is important since so much of lying is born of the

---

[*] John Calvin, *Institutes of the Christian Religion*, trans. Henry Beveridge
(2 Vols.; London: James Clarke & Co., Ltd., 1957) I, 475.

craven fear of punishment. While the liar shows contempt for the person he seeks to deceive, at the same time he is subject to apprehensiveness before him. God's forgiveness, however, exposes a man as fully known and yet forgiven. Grounds for contemptuous deceit and fear-stricken lies have been withdrawn.

There is no reason to fear that God—on the other side of his son—is something other than he reveals himself to be. He chooses to know men and to know them wholly in and through his mercy and judgment. The attempt to cover up in his presence is pointless. A man is free to be the man that he is—exposed, known, and forgiven—before him. So exposed, a man is also free to set aside the strategies of deceit with himself and his neighbor.

The strategy of self-deceit becomes pointless. If a man has no reason to hide from God, he has no further reason to hide from himself. He can be truthful with himself. He need not deceive himself with false interpretations of his past action, his present situation, or his future possibilities. It is not an accident that the first autobiography produced in the West was written by a Christian bishop, and that Augustine was able to reckon with his own life with the candor that the forgiveness of sins permits.

Self-deceit, it was observed earlier, includes a false interpretation not only of one's self, but of one's world. Therefore freedom from self-deceit means also freedom from false interpretations of one's world. This does not mean that the Christian always carries about with him an accurate picture of the world like a snapshot in his wallet. Quite the contrary, freedom from self-deceit may mean, in a given situation, a readiness to live without a picture of the world where none is forthcoming.

The strategy of neighbor-deceit also becomes pointless. If a man has no reason to hide from God, he also has no reason to hide from, or deceive, his neighbor. God's presence to a man in his word means that he can, and should, be a man of his word. There is no need to engage in a skittish dance, a giggle, or malevolence behind that word, or to hide fearfully behind a style of life—a wardrobe designed to impress.

It would be absurd, of course, to propose that men, in the name of truth, abandon all distinctions between the public and the private, the exterior and the interior. It would be adolescent to suggest that they get rid of all style in life. For style in life is nothing less than social clothing. To be honest in human affairs does not mean being unclothed.

But the exterior life of man, like clothing, ought to be expressive of the person who animates it. Not surprisingly, Scripture summarizes the whole of the ethical life by appeal to the inner man to put on the right outer clothing. In Ephesians it is reported, ". . . the truth is in Jesus." Therefore, "Put off your old nature which belongs to your former manner of life and is corrupt through deceitful lusts . . . and put on the new nature, created after the likeness of God in true righteousness and holiness" (4:21–22,24).

> Therefore, putting away falsehood, let every one speak the truth with his neighbor, for we are members one of another . . . give no opportunity to the devil . . . let no evil talk come out of your mouths, but only such as is good for edifying, as fits the occasion, that it may impart grace to those who hear. . . . Let all bitterness and wrath and anger and clamor and slander be put away from you. . . .
>
> Ephesians 4:22–31

Scripture makes no sentimental guarantee that it is simple to wear the garment of truth, but it is less complicated than the garb of the lie. Because Dante thought so, he describes a coat of lead, painted with gold, weighing down the movements of the hypocrites in hell.

10 The Dynamics of Sin:
CRAVING AND ANXIETY

Neither of the sins considered in this chapter is among the seven deadly. And yet, in the estimate of many sensitive Christians today, the second of these sins, anxiety, provides the most comprehensive context for all others. The boastfulness of the proud, the gluttony of the obese, and the obsessions of the envious have been interpreted as nothing more than ugly rubbish on the surface of a far deeper problem: man's dark undercurrent of anxiety. How could anxiety run so deep in contemporary experience and yet fail to impress the medieval moralists? (St. Thomas, for example, devotes only a side comment to anxiety in the course of a major essay on fear.) Nothing less than a sea change in religious sensibility could explain this comparative lack of interest in one age and yet obsession in another with the problem of anxiety.

Such a change has in fact taken place. St. Thomas paid little attention to the problem of anxiety for the simple reason that the medieval church interpreted the dynamics of sin in another way. Ravenous appetite (that is, concupiscence) rather than anxiety is the key to the medieval analysis of the religious situation of man. Concupiscence for the medieval theologian was not simply one sin among others, but the very dynamic of sin expressed in them all. That is why concupiscence did not have a place among the seven deadly sins. It was original sin itself, the very matrix of sin, the context in which all the others emerged. "Every sin consists in the desire for some mutable good, for which man has an inordinate desire, and the pleasure of which gives him inordinate pleasure."* With sin so defined, the medieval Christian gave almost no theological consideration to the spiritual condition of anxiety. Only with the Reformation did anxiety begin to emerge not simply as one sin among others, but rather as *the* sin, the troubled air in which other sins breathe, the dark waters on which they float.

A study of craving and anxiety forces a break in the organizational principle of this book. With the exception of deceit, each of the sins has been defined by certain specifiable relations that a man has to the world or to his fellows. The specific sin in each case has been distinguished by its most typical object.

But concupiscence and anxiety, as they will be defined here,

* *ST* I. ii. q 72 art. 2.

are distinctive in that they do not refer to particular objects but rather to an interior state of soul that precedes and complicates man's attachment to objects. Concupiscence and anxiety, in and of themselves, are objectless. This is more obvious in the case of anxiety. Contemporary writers always make a clear distinction between it and its nearest neighbor, fear. Fear is always a *fear of something*; whereas anxiety is a *dread of nothing*. Anxiety may precipitate, so to speak, into specific fears, but in itself it refers to an uneasiness of soul prior to them all. The same might be argued for concupiscence. In the nature of the case, ravenous desire attaches itself to one or more particular goods, but of itself it describes a voracity of appetite anterior to particular attachments.

It is my conviction that craving and anxiety are continuing features of man's life in sin. Neither has a constitutional priority over the other. Craving is the positive of which anxiety is the negative. Craving describes the outward, aggressive movement of the soul toward the realm of objects (although in itself it is captive to no particular object); anxiety is the soul's inward movement of withdrawal and recoil.

So defined, craving and anxiety present a contrasting pair, roughly comparable to the pairing of idolatry and faintheartedness. The man of ravenous appetite rarely avoids idolatry and the man of anxiety is an easy prey to faintheartedness. Yet craving and idolatry are not identical. While the voracity of man's appetite may lead to idolatrous attachment, the inherent restlessness of that desire may also lead to disappointment with the idol. Insatiable craving may provoke a kind of serial idolatry or, beyond idolatry, it may lead to a state of disappointment, boredom, and disinterest. In this case, ravenous desire has become its opposite: apathy. By the same token, anxiety may crystallize in the fear of certain objects, but this is not anxiety itself. A man may experience anxiety most acutely precisely at those moments when he has no enemies to fear and when success is most surely his. In brief, the objectlessness of craving and anxiety distinguishes them from the sins already analyzed. Craving is the usual matrix for the sins of idolatry, avarice, envy, and lust; and anxiety, that of faintheartedness, hatred, and betrayal. But the matrix is distinct from the objects around which life may be momentarily organized within it.

While it has been proposed here that craving and anxiety are continuing and perennial features of man's life in sin, it has also been recognized that each operates as the inclusive (and therefore somewhat exclusive) atmosphere for other sins. Each creates a climate distinct from the other, so much so that it is possible to speak of an age of desire and an age of anxiety. No better approach is available to the atmosphere of each than through the life and work of two theologians: St. Augustine and Martin Luther. We turn therefore to them for a more careful delineation of each.

St. Augustine: craving

According to the African saint, man is distinguished from all other creatures by virtue of his experience, at the very center of his being, of an infinite and boundless thirst. This is what it means to be a man. The needs of the beast, by contrast, are limited. The animal wants food, sleep, and the satisfaction of his flesh, and he sets out to meet these needs without embarrassment or complication. But unlike the animal, man knows a surplus of desire above and beyond all these "satisfactions." He can never live contentedly within their limits. At the very height of his pleasures he is thrown beyond them—whether by boredom, satiety, or an awareness of their brevity. For Augustine, this "surplus" of desire is the sign of both the grandeur and the misery of man—the grandeur of his origin and destiny, and the misery of his fall. In origin and destiny, man is intended for the satisfaction of this boundless desire that distinguishes him from the beast. God did not, in the fashion of a sadist, burden his creature with an infinite passion in order to frustrate him on every side. He created man for happiness rather than unhappiness, satisfaction rather than torture. Since an infinite passion can be satisfied only by an infinite object, man must have been created for the purpose of the satisfaction of his passion in the infinite God whose unbounded goodness, life, and power alone might provide him with perfect nourishment and rest.

This very desire, however, which distinguishes man in dignity and destiny from the beast, is at the same time the source of his misery in sin. For when man turns away from God toward the goods of this world, he attempts to satisfy an infinite passion with finite goods. He turns to what is limited, transient, and mortal, trying to satisfy therein his thirst for the eternal. For Augustine this was no mere doctrine. Looking back over his own past in the *Confessions,* he saw how he had pursued one good after another, wild with desire, seeking God all the while, painfully and mistakenly, in everything that he touched. Man seeks fulfillment in the pleasures of the flesh, but his pleasure is over in an instant. He craves fulfillment in compliments and prestige, but a few minutes after the speech is delivered and the compliment won, they lose their power to nourish. He seeks satisfaction in friends, but, alas, they disappoint. He searches for excitement in the theater, but its glory passes. He sets for himself a high ambition, difficult of achievement, but once achieved it proves lacking in substance. Augustine concluded that despite his position and the achievements of his life, he was no better off than a drunken beggar whom he saw passing along a street in Milan. ". . . For here was I striving away, dragging the load of my unhappiness under the spurring of my desires, and making it worse by dragging it: and with all our striving, our one aim was to arrive at some sort of happiness without care: the beggar had reached the same goal before us, and we might quite well never reach it at all. The very thing that he attained by means of a few pennies begged from passers-by—namely the pleasure of a temporary happiness—I was plotting for with so many a weary twist and turn." St. Augustine's reaction is one that a modern business executive or professional person might be inclined to share. "Certainly the beggar's joy was no true joy; but the joy I sought in my ambition was emptier still."

* St. Augustine, *Confessions of St. Augustine,* trans. F. J. Sheed (New York: Sheed & Ward, 1943), Bk. VI, par. vi.

In this condition Augustine reports of himself: "I strayed too far from thy sustaining power and I became to myself a barren land." The metaphor suggests that his own life, and the life of others, is a living out of the Parable of the Prodigal Son. Men leave their father's house and wander in a strange and barren land, where no substantial food can be found. Inevitably, such men are restless creatures, homeless, nomadic, wandering to and fro, putting every good that they know under the pressure of an immense longing, attempting to suck life either from themselves or from their self-appointed substitutes for God, but discovering inevitable disappointment. Augustine refers to his life as a "licking after shadows." Under these circumstances, moreover, a man not only suffers himself, he also tortures those good things to which he turns. For he tries to make them play the role of God in his life. No longer knowing how to love his wife, work, children, and possessions *in* God, he restlessly installs them *in the place of* God, and then swerves away from them in bafflement or resentment when they fail to live up to his hopeless innermost longing and expectation. At length, fatigued, disappointed, and flagged in spirit by his metaphysical misadventures, his desire itself goes dead. He becomes so hungry he cannot keep food on his stomach; so thirsty he does not thirst.

The category of desire not only provided the setting for Augustine's understanding of man as creature and sinner, it also influenced his interpretation of salvation. For Augustine—and the whole of the subsequent Catholic tradition—salvation is first and foremost a question of the recovery in Christ of the hidden object of all man's desiring, in which alone his passion is fulfilled. "O food and bread of angels!" Augustine exclaims in meditating on Christ. Impoverished man is in need of this surpassing food. The image of nourishment is prominent in Augustine's representation of the divine love. Salvation, above all else, is food from God that strengthens the soul. Grace is not so much God's forgiving love as it is his strengthening, empowering, and satisfying love. In all these matters, Augustine recalls an important element in scriptural testimony to the divine love. Admittedly, God's love is the forgiveness of his people, Israel, the father's forgiveness of the prodigal, the Lord's forgiveness of sins in the shedding of his blood. But just as much, God's love is power and food. It is manna in the wilderness. It is the fatted calf killed. It is the Lord's body broken and shared in a sacrament whose model is the lowly act of eating. Salvation is always a receiving of those good things in which alone man's desire can be filled.

Craving as a sin and the several sins

In the context of Christian thought, desire, as such, is clearly not sinful. This distinguishes Christianity from Stoicism and from certain Eastern traditions in which desire is evil and its attrition necessary for salvation. A state of desirelessness is not the Christian ideal. The tradition totally rejected the stoic ideal of passionlessness, when it identified sloth—understood as apathy —as one of the seven capital sins.

Three phenomena must be distinguished: creaturely desire, craving, and finally, craving as it is pluralized among the several sins. Creaturely desire—for God and one's fellow—in itself is good. It is proof that man is not, by origin and destiny, an occluded monad. He is intended for God and his fellow (and not simply for dutiful service but for enjoyment and satisfaction in both).

Craving is complicated both with reference to creaturely desire and to the pluralization of the sins. In one sense, the energy of craving is constitutive and creaturely rather than sinful. It is the mark of God on the creature. It gives evidence of a man's sense of the lack of God in the urgency and restlessness with which he pursues finite goods. And yet, at the same time, craving is not a pure expression of creaturely desire. The restless objectlessness of craving already indicates a state of removal from God. No longer is man a creature with an infinite passion (in the sense of a passion for the Infinite); rather, his passion infinitizes itself. It suffers a loss of boundaries as it seeks without limit to satisfy itself.

Craving is also complicated with respect to finite goods. On the one hand, it is the basis for the pluralization of the sins, for craving propels man toward mutable goods. This is the aspect of concupiscence that the medieval tradition emphasizes. In the act in which man chooses to reject God, he does so only for the sake of some lesser good. He never chooses—even when he sins—*evil for its own sake.* When he moves *away* from God, he moves *toward* some attractive object. Within the matrix of craving, then, the various particular sins are distinguished from one another on the basis of the specific good that each offers in the place of God. This is pre-eminently the case with the seven capital sins. Each offers a certain distinctive good that is desirable, and which can give rise to a whole way of life—and vice—organized around that good. Thus avarice is an inordinate love of money; vainglory, the desire for reputation; lust, for sex and the pleasures of touch; gluttony, for food; anger, for revenge; and the queen of them all, pride, an inordinate craving for excellence.*

Although craving propels man toward finite goods, it can also be the basis for his alienation from them. This is the aspect of concupiscence that the medieval tradition overlooks, but to which the experience of men attests. It is the basis for our assertion that craving finally is objectless. Pascal, as well as St. Augustine, recognized this when they observed that man alternates between raging desire and bored satiety. This accounts for a man's capacity for serial idolatry—the restless movement from good to good in quest for what he knows not. It also accounts for the peculiar dynamics of perversion, at the secret center of which is boredom with the sexual object. Driven by boredom, the pervert requires an endless variation in technique or an exquisite refinement of pleasure until his pleasure is abstracted from the full-bodied object. He leaves the sexual object discarded on a slag heap. This analysis of craving as objectless also accounts for the sadism to which Augustine obliquely refers when he distinguishes between the *use* and *abuse* of finite goods.

* Pride does not figure as one of the seven capital sins according to St. Thomas. Rather it is the primordial sin from which the others are descended, the capital of the capitals. Among the seven, vainglory most closely resembles it.

If I place my wife under the pressure of being a redeemer-figure in my life, or demand from my children an extravagant accomplishment to atone for my own mediocre achievements, my craving, in effect, is objectless. I crave neither the God that is nor the wife and children that can be. My craving has an object only in fancy and I abuse reality accordingly. I try to force my wife and children into a role that ought not and cannot be theirs. If it is replied that desire does indeed have an object in these cases, an object in fancy rather than in fact (just as fears may be directed to real or imaginary objects), then let it be proposed that craving, like anxiety, may be the boundless, formless dynamic abyss from which the tortured and torturing shapes of desire and fear emerge. Finally, the objectlessness of craving explains how the movement toward the idol may proceed beyond the idol to that state of boredom and disinterest which the medieval world knew so well as the sin of sloth. The slothful man is the apathetic man. He is medieval man in his extremity. His desire for all particular goods is dead.

Martin Luther: anxiety

The medieval theologian could imagine the dead end of craving in the slump of sloth, but not its reduction to a place of secondary significance. This is what happened with the change in religious atmosphere that set in with the Protestant Reformers. Concupiscence as a term still figured in theological discourse, but anxiety replaced craving as the setting and context for the several sins. Correspondingly, the term "assurance" (rather than "satisfaction") was the key to man's quest for salvation.

Perhaps there is no more economical way to recall the plight of the young Martin Luther and his quest for assurance before God than to consider St. Thomas' own brief remarks on anxiety as a species of fear. According to Aquinas, the peculiar characteristic of fear is that it is directed to a future evil (as opposed, for example, to sorrow, which is directed toward a past, or present, evil). Fear modifies into anxiety whenever this evil cannot be fully foreseen. An element of uncertainty immediately obtrudes itself into the situation, producing a certain uneasiness in man. This uneasy fear is nothing other than anxiety—man's affective state insofar as he relates to a future evil that is unforeseen and, in the nature of the case, unforeseeable.

St. Thomas does not do full justice to the experience of anxiety, but his remarks help interpret the religious quest of the young Martin Luther.

Luther, above all else, was a man seeking salvation. He sought communion with God. The church of his time declared that communion with God was indeed the future of the Christian man, if he made use of the specific ways and means to salvation available through its laws and the sacraments. The way to salvation was obedience to the law of God, as it was expressed and elaborated in the special rules and discipline of the church. The ordinary means to salvation was the grace of God contained in the sacraments of the church. Through participation in the sacraments the individual Christian received power which would help him to obey the law of God and thus prepare himself for eventual and eternal communion with God. The church said, in effect, "Take these sacraments and obey these laws and you will win eternal life in the presence of God."

Luther tried every means that was available at his time to seek assurance before God. As a priest, he made full use of the sacraments and the sacramentals. He attended seriously to the Sermon on the Mount and tried to live up to its commandments; and he made use of the confessional, so much so that his confessor accused him of the sin of scrupulosity. But across all his efforts to seek assurance before God must be written the two Latin words *Deus absconditus*—God is hidden. None of his efforts was capable of producing the face of God and assuring him of divine favor. Indeed, his own efforts to live by the law of God only served to multiply his doubts. When confronted by the Sermon on the Mount, Luther was engulfed by a sense of his failure to live by its commandments. Jesus had said, "Have no anxiety about anything." But what was his life except anxious? Jesus had said that whoever looks at a woman with lust in his heart has already committed adultery with her. Measured against this command, what man could escape condemnation? But even when Luther succeeded in obeying the law, he found himself falling into further difficulties. If he avoided the sins of unrighteousness, he fell into the sins of self-righteousness. If he avoided the sins of the publicans, he fell into the sins of the pharisees. His good works were no more useful to him than his evil works in attaining to the presence of God. In fact, Luther came to the conclusion that all his efforts at salvation through his own works actually removed him further from the presence of God, because they were all headed in the wrong direction. They were efforts at self-justification. These actions only served to drive him deeper into himself, away from God, as he used them to contrive some sort of security before God. Meanwhile God himself became more and more the hidden enemy whom he tried to appease. Every act of self-justification already presupposed that he was trying to put himself to rights with an unfriendly power. Instead of bringing him closer to God, all his efforts merely attested to and intensified his sense of estrangement.

Luther discovered, in brief, that the path that the medieval church had marked out so confidently as leading to salvation ended in a question mark. God's future judgment upon the sinner is in doubt. God becomes an X, an unknown. All systems of self-salvation collapse in a final agnosticism about the favor of God. They produce that uneasy fear to which St. Thomas referred. What is the decision of God on the Day of Judgment? A Yes? A No? A Maybe? On the basis of the law of God: most likely, a No.

Only at this point in his life did Luther come to realize that the church was ignoring the very substance of the Christian message in which alone he might find assurance of God's favor. Luther turned, in effect, from the laws to the promises of God contained in Scripture and he found in these promises alone the assurances that none of his own efforts could provide. Luther discovered that God, as he has actually made himself known to men in the testimony of Scripture, is not an X lurking in the future, upon whose final word men wait uneasily. Rather, he has already spoken an immovable word of assurance to sinners in the past. Specifically, he is the God of Abraham, Isaac, and Jacob, who promised himself to his people at Mt. Sinai and who fulfilled this promise to men in the sending of his Son. God's word to man is not a word of judgment alone, but above all else a word of assurance to the sinner that his sins are forgiven and that all grounds for his anxiety before God have been set aside.

In Christ, the sign of God's unconditional favor has been set down in the midst of men. Men were once like sons trying to talk to a father whose face was hidden. But now the distance between the father and the son has been overcome by the decisive act in which the father shows his hand and his face, so that once and for all the son stands assured of his favor. Man's assurance of salvation rests upon the faithfulness of God to man in Christ. Man is forgiven by God for all his sins of unrighteousness and self-righteousness, and even for that anxious distrust in the promises of God from which these sins proceed. Because this is the case, he can afford to put aside all the little stratagems of anxiety. In Luther's time, this meant specifically that men could renounce all those actions which they previously performed so feverishly or indolently to win God's favor: heroic prayers, appeals to the saints, pilgrimages to Rome, lonely fastings, and ecclesiastical splendors. In modern times, it means that men can afford to put aside their own preferred means of self-justification: the accumulation of money, the dignity of a career, the moisture in one's passions, or the subtlety of one's opinions. Having put aside all these works, stripped clean of everything except the assurance of God's grace, a man can truly begin to live freely and lightheartedly, obedient to God and servant to his neighbor. In brief, it was Luther's rediscovery that assurance is not an uncertain destination; it is the indispensable, wholly surpriseful and merciful point of departure in the Christian life.

Further development of the problem of anxiety and assurance in its Reformation context would require moving beyond the idiom of Luther to that of Calvin. The problem of assurance leads inevitably to the doctrine of predestination. Calvin's doctrine of predestination, understood in its positive aspect, was a way of saying that the forgiveness of sins was no passing event. It was rooted in eternity. Because it was rooted in his eternal will, God's forgiveness could really be trusted. There was no reason for an uneasy fear that God would change his mind. The great irony of Calvinism was that it combatted the agnosticism of medieval Catholicism about the future judgment of God, only to fall into an agnosticism of its own about the past action of God. With its doctrine of the secret decrees of God, laid up before the beginning of the world, Calvinism substituted for an X in the future its own X in the past. Calvin and Calvinists, just as surely as the medieval church, forgot that: ". . . the Son of God, Jesus Christ, whom we preached among you . . . was not Yes and No; but in him it is always Yes. For all the promises of God find their Yes in him" (II Corinthians 1:19–20).

Anxiety and the several sins

Neither Luther nor other theologians of the sixteenth century explicitly reinterpreted the various sins in the context of anxiety. It remained for theologians of the nineteenth and twentieth centuries to do this. The key terms in any such reinterpretation are uncertainty and insecurity. Men turn to powers other than God not so much because they are desirable but because they offer some relief from insecurity. The proud man clings to his intellectual, social, moral, or spiritual attainments not for the satisfactions which they offer as attractive goods, but for the se-curities which they provide for his own threatened existence.* The avaricious man clings to his possessions not because a good lies shining before him in the foreground of his life, but because some uncertainty menaces him from the background and drives him for assurance to his possessions. Apparently the hands of the avaricious no longer tremble with desire to hold a precious object in their grasp; rather they cling to the object in order to keep

* See Reinhold Niebuhr, *Nature and Destiny of Man: A Christian Interpreta-tion* (2 Pts.; London: Nisbet, 1941), Pt. I, chap. vii, for the analysis of pride in the context of anxiety and insecurity.

from trembling! And so it goes with the remainder of the sins.
The gluttonous man turns to his food, the lustful man to his
sexuality, the wrathful man to his obsessions, the slothful man to
his depression, and the envious man to his sorrow; each finds
therein an ordering of his life which may not delight but which
relieves him of the burden of an uncertain life before God.

It is the lovelessness of the motive in each case that is particularly striking in the modern experience and interpretation of the
sins. Men turn to careers and possessions with loveless fervor in
order to secure their lives against the impalpable. Whether it is a
question of the compulsive eater or spender, each is motivated
less by desire than by uneasiness and tension. The diverse faulted,
human activities are defensive reactions against insecurity rather
than positive drives toward pleasure.

No man, of course, can provide himself with a life wholly free
of uncertainty. The avaricious man, after all, may seek to secure
himself by means of possessions, but he can never protect himself
entirely from the uncertainties that plague his relation to them.
But he prefers these secondary uncertainties to the primary uncertainty of life alone before God. They are more bearable. At
least they have their focus in a possession that is known. But in
the case of God, it is God himself about whom man cannot be
sure. Thus man readily exchanges the primary uncertainties of
his relationship to God for the secondary awkwardnesses of his
relations to money, a woman, or a luxurious life.

Is anxiety a sin?

Even were it admitted that anxiety has become the atmosphere
and context for other sins, the question still remains as to
whether anxiety itself is a sin. Quite apart from psychoanalytic
literature, theological reflection on the subject of anxiety forces
the question. Is not anxiety existential rather than sinful? Is it
not an inevitable condition of the creaturely existence of man, a
fatal coefficient of his freedom, creativity, and mortality, and not
itself a violation of that condition? Since Kierkegaard, many

theologians and philosophers have recognized anxiety as the comprehensive context for sin, but they have not interpreted anxiety itself as sin. Although they have recognized the sinful nature of certain secondary emotions, such as a "destructive" or "neurotic" anxiety and a craven fear, they have understood anxiety itself, at its deepest level, as being embedded in human existence itself and not a declension from that existence. Indeed, for some theologians such anxiety, far from being sinful, is actually privileged among the emotions. It unveils a man to himself; it forces him to face himself as the free, creative, and mortal being that he is.

Anxiety is that state of mind in which man is laid open to the uncertainty which inwardly characterizes his existence and which sets him apart from other beings. Apart from anxiety, the existentialists argue, a man does not know himself as distinct from the animal. He interprets himself as a being endowed with a specific nature and with a corresponding set of needs and satisfactions that mark its fulfillment. Human existence is then interpreted through the reflected light of a theory more appropriate to animal life. This theory is inadequate because man is peculiarly and disruptively characterized by his freedom. This freedom is misunderstood when it is reduced to an element or factor within man's nature rather than recognized as that through which man is thrown *beyond* the certitudes of a nature. Man is an ecstatic being. Literally, he stands outside of any given determination of himself and his "needs," as he projects himself daily into the uncertainty of his own future. The language is that of Heidegger and Sartre, but it is not far removed from the terms of the theologians when they have referred to man as a self-transcendent being. Unlike the animal, man travels beyond previous determinations of himself. This constant traveling beyond himself means that uncertainty is not something that limits human existence from without; rather it marks it from within.

Uncertainty, of course, marks human existence not only by virtue of the fact that man is free, but also in that he is a free being who dies. His death, moreover, is radically distinct from the perishing of an animal, for man *knows* that he dies and knows that his dying is uncertain as to its hour. Man cannot relate properly to such a death as an event external to his existence. Death penetrates his existence from within with uncertainty. It cuts unexpectedly across the pursuit of his most cherished goals, depriving him of that absolute assurance with which he would like to pursue his life aims. Nor should man seek to evade this uncertainty which marks him as a free creature who dies. Man is himself only insofar as he lives at the center of this uncertainty, taking upon himself the full dread of his freedom and death.

This existentialist intepretation of anxiety raises the question whether anxiety is properly understood as a sin or simply as an affective state entirely appropriate to the creaturely condition of man. One possibility would be to distinguish anxiety before God (as Luther understood it) and anxiety before one's own freedom and death (as the modern existentialists describe it) and to restrict the sin of anxiety to the former alone.

Sinful anxiety then would refer only to anxiety before God: specifically, to uncertainty about the favor of God. The sin would be an act of distrust in the promises that God himself has already given. When man thinks of God as an X lurking in the future, before whom he has to make a good showing, he is acting as if God has not spoken unconditional words of assurance and pardon to himself as a sinner. He tries to transfer the question of assurance to his own hands. He fails to accept the fact that his own existence is not rendered doubtful just because it is in God's hands. He refuses to accept the contingency of his existence with assurance. Quite literally, the contingency of existence means that it "touches upon" another. For the anxious man, this contingency means that everything has become touch and go. He feels compelled to shore up his life on some other basis than God. This is the specific anxiety which is at the root of all other sins.

By confining sinful anxiety in this fashion to the God relationship, one is free to accept the existentialist analysis of anxiety before freedom and death without confusing the latter phenomena with sin. Trust in the promises of God would not rule out altogether an anguished sense of an X in life. It would not render everything else transparent. There could still be an anguished sense of uncertainty before one's self and the uses of one's freedom even though one's destiny before God is assured. There could still be genuine uncertainty before the neighbor who stands opaque and unfathomable over and against one's self. There could still be dread in the dark, uneasiness in the forest, a vertigo in the heights, and a trembling before one's own fate and death. These uncertainties would neither be ruled out by creation nor excluded by salvation. They belong to human existence itself and could not be called, when apprehended with dread, sin.

The foregoing distinction between sinful anxiety and existential anxiety has the advantage of restricting the term "sin" to those who have heard the promises of God (whether explicitly or implicitly in their lives) and distrusted them. It maintains the confessional boundaries of the term "sin." It does not put the Christian in the foolish position of claiming that the anxieties that Heidegger, Sartre, and Freud describe are a case of sin for all men. Quite properly, the Christian renounces clairvoyance on the subject of another man's life before God and his promises.

However, this refusal to extend the term "sin" into a general anthropology does not mean conversely that the Christian himself is free to distinguish between his own anxiety before God and his anxiety in facing the world, and to reserve the term "sin" for the former alone. Assurance before God is empty if it is not also assurance for a man as he takes up his daily responsibilities in the flesh. This is the arena in which his assurance before God is tested. A Christian does not fully trust in God if he is anxious before his boss, worried about his children, and in dread before his death. Nor does he trust in God (and this is the point at which this argument breaks with the existentialists) if he treats his own freedom and futurity in the world as a mere X without content or specification.

The interpretation of sin, as well as that of salvation, is flawed with angelism if either anxiety or assurance is restricted to the God relationship alone. A man's relationship to God cannot be abstracted from his ties by flesh and spirit to his world. Assurance before God is assurance in the world. Christ himself makes it difficult for the Christian to withdraw from the human arena. When the Christian turns toward God, he faces a Lord who entered into the world, suffered it, and made it his own. He is confronted then by a promise from God that is not just God but the world. For this reason Paul does not urge restrictively: "Have no anxiety before God"; but rather, "Have no anxiety about anything".*

This is not to conclude, however, that the Christian experiences in this life a perfect assurance before God and the world. In the light of the directive from Paul, who could claim it? Even the theologian who insisted most vehemently on the element of assurance in the Christian life was compelled to write: "When we say that faith must be certain and secure, we certainly speak not of an assurance which is never affected by doubt, nor a security which anxiety never assails, we rather maintain that believers have a perpetual struggle with their own distrust. . . ." This is not to say, on the other hand, that nothing has been accomplished in the faithful by the promises in Christ. ". . . Whatever be the mode in which they are assailed, we deny that they fall off and abandon that sure confidence which they have formed in the mercy of God." Or again, Calvin writes "Though we are agitated and carried to and fro by distrust, we are not immediately plunged into the abyss; though we are shaken, we are not therefore driven from our place."**

Anguish before God and the world may not be fully erased for the man of faith, but two responses to his anguish are rendered superfluous. First, he is relieved of the Philistine's need to flee into securities other than the promises of God. He does not need to bind himself over to idols in order to win heart's ease from his anxieties. He can begin to reckon with the darkness, the forest, and the heights; he can begin to contend with his own threaten-

---

* Philippians 4:6.
** John Calvin, *Institutes of the Christian Religion*, trans. Henry Beveridge (2 vols.; London: James Clarke & Co. Ltd., 1957), I, 484, 486.

ing freedom and that of his neighbors; he does not need to turn away nervously from his own fate and death. These experiences of a dreadful X in his life are now limited by the promises of God who extended himself in human form into the world. They do not open out on an unbearable darkness.

But second, and just as surely, the Christian is freed from the opposite temptation of some of the existentialists who, stifled and repelled by the idols of the Philistines, turn away from their confining securities and embrace the dreadful night as though it were God. Man does not need to worship the mysteries of the forest in order to be free of the city; the mountains, to be free of the plains; death, to be free of life; and the uncertainties of freedom, to be free of its trivial uses. God's promises limit a man without stifling him, give him assurance without banishing mystery. Therefore, he is freed from the need to flee from their limit and their assurance as though to recover his own soul in the spaciousness of the night.

The order of priority between craving and anxiety

The assumption has been made both by the classical tradition and by modern existentialists that there is an order of priority between craving and anxiety. Clearly, for the classical tradition, craving is primary and anxiety quite secondary. Anxiety is but a species of fear. Only in the context of man's love of certain objects is it possible for him to fear other objects. And only insofar as this fear is directed toward a future evil whose consummation is uncertain does anxiety come into play. Clearly, anxiety has a derivative relationship to desire.

For the existentalists, on the other hand, desire is wholly subordinate to anxiety. The latter is privileged among emotions as it opens man to that uncertainty which he himself *is* in the depths of his being. All other emotions (including those of desire and fear) have a strictly secondary, derivative, and privative significance. Fear and desire, indeed, are taken as primary emotions only insofar as man finds the uncertainty of his being unbearable and wrongly interprets himself as an animal "nature" with given wants and certain definable ends. In the existentialist interpretation, the sin of all sins is not the immoderate desire for certain ends—such as sex, money, or food. Rather, it is man's yielding to the temptation to interpret himself in terms of the category of desire in the first place. This is the original sin from which all others flow. Man understands himself in terms of the apparent certainties of a nature, its desires and satisfactions, and he flees from his high calling as a free being.

In this essay, no attempt has been made to rank craving over anxiety, or vice versa, in the phenomenology of sin. Anxiety has been interpreted as the negative of which craving is the positive. In the course of this insistence on their polar relationship to one another, craving has been redefined in such a way as to bring it somewhat more parallel to the existentialist definition of anxiety. But there is no particular reason to assign one sin pre-eminence over the other. Indeed, the Christian cannot do without a double sense of the love of God—both the father's forgiveness and his feeding of the prodigal son. The Christian experience of salvation comprehends both. It is impoverished if either is lacking.

If the ancient Catholic consciousness of craving served to remind the Christian that grace is food from God, then the modern consciousness of anxiety should serve to remind him that grace is pardon from God. Without the assurance of pardon, the fatted calf is inedible. The celebration meal is stricken with uncertainties as to why it has occurred, with whom, and for how long. It is a prisoner's table, a stranger's handout, and not the celebration of a father with his dead son. For considerations such as these, anxiety and craving should be considered together as the dynamics and atmosphere of sin.

The
Destination of Sin

11 The Shadow of Solitude:
PRIDE

Why put a chapter on pride toward the end of a book on the
several sins? According to tradition, pride belongs at the beginning. Ranked first, pride is neither an overestimation of one's
talent (egotism), nor a flutter of delight that goes with accomplishment (vanity), nor an inner firmness of identity that is essential to integrity (self-respect); it means, rather, man's self-
exaltation into the position of God. Pride is nothing less than the
human imagination fully seized by the Tempter's beautiful
promise, "You will be like God," and the ugly fruition of this
promise in the swollen, the murderous, and the devious heart.

So defined, pride held first place among the sins, not only
chronologically but generatively. Out of respect for its generative
power, the church tradition ranked pride not merely first *among*,
but first *ahead of* the seven capital sins (vainglory taking its
place among the seven) so as to express the conviction that it was
the very capital of the capital sins, the ruling queen among her
attendants. Pride had an original and generative relationship
even to those sins that generated others.

Still, there is a further truth about pride that only its place-

ment toward the end of this book will serve to underscore. Pride
functions as the beginning of the various sins only because it also
looms ahead as their finished result, their final destination; and
therefore gives inner direction to their work along the way.

The end result of each of the sins in its extremity is solitude
and death. This is the inner logic and unimpeded destiny of
them all. Avarice, malice, neglect, lust, deceit and others all
move in the direction of the occluded self, the self shut off not
only from God but from the world and the neighbor. This is the
self whose terminal connections with God, the world, and the
neighbor have gone dead. But this double destiny of solitude and
death is not so clear when the sins are considered in and of
themselves apart from their extremity. Only in the specific sins of
pride and sloth does the destiny of them all unfold.

In each sin, man turns away from God as the center of his life.
But in most he does not reach the state of the occluded or the
dead self. God has fallen away from the horizon of the sinner but
creation has not. The idolator, for example, denies God but he
does not abandon the creation in its entirety. On the contrary, he
clings to some lustrous fragment of the creation, raised to the
power of God. Similarly, the lustful, the avaricious, the gluttonous, and so forth, no matter how occluded in other respects
their behavior may be, do not allow the creation to slip entirely
from view. Pride, however, is that sin in which not only God but
the creation has fallen away and the self is left to itself alone.
Pride is the sin of the first person singular. It is not yet an
absolute, unrelieved, and uninterrupted solitude, but it is certainly the shadow of that solitude. The daydreams of pride are
solitary. All other persons, numbers, and genders bow down before it—like the sheaves in Joseph's dream—while only the first
person singular remains.

The essence of pride

Pride is self-devotion, self-justification, and self-glorying in
contempt of God. In this respect, we do not wish to alter St.
Augustine's definition of pride as "the love of self in contempt of

God." The word "contempt" in this definition need not be limited to those who sustain a controversy against God, deliberately insulting and contemning his name. Our own best equivalent might be "aversion." In pride man is averse to the existence of God. He would find his existence an unwelcome intrusion in his life—uncomfortable, irritating, and hopelessly confining. God must be treated with that contempt an adult displays toward a child when he is annoyed by his intrusion into a conversation. At all costs, some way must be found to ignore the intruder, or to brush him aside, or to shunt him off into the next room, while the proper themes of adult life—the building of careers, the tearing down of reputations, the consoling of egos, the strengthening of opinions—are pursued. Just as surely as the intrusion of a child disrupts the bases of adult conversation, the presence of God appears an awkward disruption of the various monologues and dialogues promoted by the God-isolated self. Rather than suffer a radical revision in the themes of his conversation, the proud man is altogether more comfortable finding a way to divert attention from the voice of an intruder. Pride is simply a matter of cleaving to the self and its loves and fears in such a way as to be cold and dead and averse to the presence of God.

This aversion to God is more than an emotional state of irritation with God and his existence. The prideful man lives and moves on a course of head-on collision with his Maker and Savior. That is why the church has not hesitated to use the strongest metaphors drawn from the sphere of politics to describe this state of radical opposition to God. Pride is rebellion against God; it is warfare against the divine being. Not to be overlooked, however, is the metaphor of height. The direction of pride is upward against the divine being. Pride is self-exaltation. It is a preference for heights. The Latin term *superbia* refers to an overreaching of the self, a stepping forward and out of place—not just a few feet, but into the place of God. "And what is pride but a perverse desire of height, in forsaking Him to whom the soul ought solely to cleave, as the beginning thereof, to make it seem its own beginning."[*]

[*] St. Augustine, *City of God*, ed. R. V. G. Tasker (2 Vols.; London: J. M. Dent and Sons, 1945), Bk. XIV, chap. xiii.

This spatial image for pride is susceptible to two different interpretations, at the extreme of which are the Greek and Christian understandings of the sin. Obviously the image assumes, even though in an unspecified way, that God is above and man below. The opposition is one of competition. Man competes with God by seeking to rise above his place into the place of God. The purest example of this interpretation of pride is found in the Greek concept of *hubris*. Prometheus is guilty of stealing fire from the gods. He reaches upward to take possession of the very substance and power of divinity. Since man needs divine fire in order to be fully himself, a creative man, there is an element of tragic necessity in this warfare between Promethean man and the gods. To exist is to sin. Human creativity unavoidably places man in tension with heavenly powers, whose reaction is prompt, brutal, and unrelenting against his show of ambition.

This interpretation of pride is partly accepted and partly rejected in the Christian tradition. On the whole, the theologians relieved pride of the tragic necessity it held for the Greeks but they still tended to think in terms of the same spatial model. Pride is simply reinterpreted as a wholly unjustified pretension on the part of man to live above the line that distinguishes the creature from the Creator. It is possible for man to be fully himself, a man, without usurping the attributes and prerogatives of divinity. St. Augustine, therefore, was typical of the classical theologians when he observed that the proud man seeks gratuitously and grotesquely to imitate God. The sinner is engaged in a perverse mimicry of the divine being. In fact, each of the sins emanating from pride, is a grotesque parody of one of the perfections of God. Curiosity imitates God's omniscience; ambition seeks to duplicate God's glory; luxuriousness parodies the abundance of the divine life, and so forth. In each case, the proud man seeks to appropriate to himself those perfections that belong to God alone. This analysis presupposes, of course, that the proud man actually has a clear notion of the divine omniscience, omnipotence, glory, and so forth, and that his perversity lies in their forbidden appropriation.

There is a second use of the spatial metaphor in the Christian tradition that represents an advance on the first. According to this model, pride is a contradiction of God, not because God is fixedly above, and man below (this is a picture of the situation already determined by a Luciferian envy of God). Rather, pride contradicts God because it moves upward, in contradiction to God's movement downward. This movement in opposite directions results in a head-on collision between God and man. While man shows a preference for heights, the Son of man came into the depths; while man strives to prove his righteousness, the Son of man assumed unrighteousness. So understood, the man of pride does not really compete for a power that belongs properly to God himself. He misunderstands that power as it is disclosed in the humiliation of Jesus Christ. The power of the Cross contradicts his daydreams concerning divine power.

This interpretation of the sin is as old as the Scriptures but it has had its most recent radical statement in the work of the theologian Karl Barth.* According to Barth, pride must be seen as a pretension to heights which is not really directed to God in his true power but rather to God as he has already been misinterpreted by the fancy of the prideful imagination. For God is not all-powerful, all-knowing, beneficent, and glorious as pride understands these perfections. He may have all these attributes, but only as they have been redefined in that event in which God has moved toward man in Jesus Christ. This movement of humiliation disturbs and contradicts pride's picture of an aloof, enviable deity.

The contradiction between Olympian deity and Promethean man is nothing compared with the opposition between the God of Jesus Christ and the man of pride. The Olympian god and the Promethean, after all, share something in common—their love of heights. A quarrel between them takes on the color of a squabble among children. But what is it that the man of pride wants from the Christian God? He is confronted by an omnipotence that stoops; he is baffled by an omniscience that assumes the darkness of Good Friday. His images of sublimity are contradicted. If he

* Karl Barth, *Church Dogmatics*, ed. G. W. Bromiley and T. F. Torrance (12 Vols.; Edinburgh: T. & T. Clark, 1956), Vol. IV, Pt. I, par. 60; Pt. II.

aims to be an eminent king, teacher, or physician he is disturbingly confronted by a figure who, at the end of his life, is a king with no subjects, a teacher with no pupils, a healer who bleeds. If he is ever to know life with this God, then he must himself be killed. That is the true meaning of the deadliness of his sin. Pride is deadly not because it produces murder—though it may —and not because it may produce future punishment at the hands of God—though this may be deserved—but because the man of pride himself must altogether die as the man he is. He must be crucified with Christ. His contradiction of God must be contradicted, his direction altogether reversed; he must be sent sprawling from his foothold on the side of the mountain to whose top he aspires. This is the terrifying import of the fact that the Son of God did not choose to dwell at the top of Mt. Olympus, but rather to die on Mt. Golgotha. His choice was altogether the downward sweep of a suffering love, but a love that kills.

This second Christian restatement of the spatial metaphor has its own difficulty. Its awkwardness has nothing to do with spatiality as such, but rather with the vertical image of "above and below." The image has unfortunate spiritual associations. A downward movement of love, after all, more than faintly suggests condescension; and condescension itself is one of the modes of pride. It is ironical then to represent the contradiction of pride in an act that appears to express pride. No metaphor escapes its own peculiar set of difficulties. But perhaps on the subject of pride (that is, on the subject of the occluded self) theology should have resort to a different kind of spatial imagery: not from above downward but from within outward. God is not himself a withdrawn, isolated monad. In his own being, he is Father, Son, and Holy Spirit. Within the divine life there is movement from one to another, from within to without. Generation, communication, and communion, rather than occlusion, characterize the inner life of God. This is why the events of creation and redemption cannot be interpreted as contrary to divine power. The God who is already other than himself within himself now lets there be reality other than himself outside himself. And when his creatures withdraw into themselves and away from one another, he re-establishes openness, communication, and communion with them in the exposure of the divine love. Christ, then, is the divine love *exposed* rather than *superimposed* from above. This love at once contradicts the centripetal movement of pride and extends itself into the arena which God chooses not to forsake.

The characteristics of pride:
Its generative power and its invisibility

Pride is the beginning of all sin in that it generates others. The act of self-assertion in which man attempts to be his own lord produces various sins against the neighbor and against the truth. This generative power of pride is not that of a discrete sin among others. Rather pride is the beginning of all sin in the sense that it is the vital power, the continuing principle in each. In a sense, all other sins are but the expression of pride. Wrapped up in malice, neglect, lust, gluttony, and envy is the self-preoccupied self. But this is precisely what is obscure in the other sins, particularly in those in which man is under the thrall of a power outside himself. As it has already been pointed out, the element of religious obsession in idolatry, faintheartedness, malice, and envy would make it appear that man is merely the passive victim in each. He seems neither responsible nor guilty for his sin. The self-assertion in his act has taken on a certain protective coloration from the power into which he is absorbed. Surely there is an element of helpless reflex in the dance of the Israelites around the golden calf, or in their fearful recoil before the power of the Amorites, or in the hapless envy and rage of King Saul. In this sense, other sins are not simply the expressions of pride, but function as the disguises of pride. Not until sin reaches its destination in the solitary self does it become wholly clear that self-assertion has had its part in its beginning. In placing pride first among the sins, the church insisted that man is responsible for his sin, that man, in fact, is guilty in his sin, and that sin is sin and not religious fate.

No attempt will be made to sketch out the many faces of pride. A discussion of those various sins it produces would involve one in a recapitulation of this book and more. But there remains the task of showing the inner connection between pride and the several sins. Perhaps it can be suggested by recalling only a few.

First, and most conspicuously, rebellion against God can produce simple aggression against one's fellow man. Augustine found this truth written into the very genealogy of the Old Testament. Proud Adam begets the murderer Cain. The vertical sin of pride produces the horizontals of envy, malice, lying, betrayal and suspicion against the brother.

If I reject God as the Lord of my life, I am free now to deny him as Lord of my brother. Having rejected him as Lord of my brother, I am free now, and tempted, to become my brother's lord, judging him in envy, managing him in lying, undercutting him in betrayal, or destroying him in malice. The Lord is no longer an obstacle between us, no longer the gift binding us together. I reject him as such and feel free to play the role of the enemy against my brother. Not only am I free to sin against the brother in this way, but pride persuades me that I am compelled to do so. (It is this element of compulsion in the relation of pride to the other sins that moved St. Thomas to observe that sin can be the cause of sin.) In pride I have elected to be my own sovereign. I feel constrained, therefore, to suspect and reject every threat to my dominion. "For he that glories in dominion must needs see his glory diminished when he has a partner to share with him."[*] I am disposed to regard my neighbor as a threat to my dominion, or to reduce him to a territory whose conquest is evidence of my dominion. Who will credit my assumption that mine is the kingdom, the power, and the glory, unless I enlarge the borders of my kingdom, the magnitude of my power, and the brightness of my glory? The *pride* of pride demands successes at the neighbor's expense.

This pressure for success at the neighbor's expense is rooted in the very failure of pride to occupy the place of God. As it was

[*] St. Augustine, *op. cit.*, Vol. II, bk. XV, chap. v.

pointed out earlier, pride seeks, but does not know how to find, the throne of God to contend with. It seeks the Highest among the highest, the Lord among the lords, and not the Highest among the lowest, the Lord among the servants to whom he has come. Pride is threatened not so much by God's limiting presence as by his unsearchable absence. Unable to locate his throne, the man of pride settles for the thrones of others, seeking to raid, invade, and subvert them, as proof of the success of his seizure of power. These compensatory proofs that pride demands of its power are illustrated with a vengeance in the legends about Satan. The failure of his rebellion against God prepares the way for his warfare against God's creatures. Pride produces its secondary sins of envy, malice, avarice, betrayal, and lust.

The strategy of warfare, however, is not the only option available to pride. It is also possible to enlarge a kingdom by way of peaceful annexation. Why destroy my neighbor with malice, if I can suffocate him with philanthropy? Why topple his monuments, if I can get him to build a monument to me? Why prove my invincibility against an enemy when it is possible to become indispensable to him as a friend? Let me shower my neighbor with wisdom, advice, and benefits to prove what a fount of goodness has its source in me. These are the quieter ways of pride that appeal to the respected, the loved, and the established—teacher, minister, benefactor, and parent—as they attempt, just as surely as the ruthless and the violent, to exalt themselves into the position of a god. The purposes of pride can be accomplished not only by aggression but by philanthropy, not only by a young and ruthless Caesar, but also by an aging benefactor and statesman who enlarges the borders of his kingdom by way of peaceful annexation.

There is yet a third reflex of pride in its relations to the neighbor. Herein a man tries to prove the success of his movement against God, not so much by a movement against his neighbor (as in warfare), nor by a movement over his neighbor (as in philanthropy), but by a withdrawal apart from his neighbor. The medieval term for this movement of withdrawal was "singularity"; the usual modern expressions are aloofness, self-righteous-

ness, or, simply, snobbery. Whatever the term, the methods of
warfare and peaceful annexation have been renounced. Both
involve too much "body contact" with the neighbor (whether
too much hand-to-hand combat or too much handshaking). The
man who dislikes body contact opts neither for warfare, nor annexation, but for a politics of secession.

The medieval moralist and mystic, Bernard, offered keen insight
into this aspect of pride under the category of "singularity." His
portrait of the sin, of course, was sketched out in the social context of the monastery. The proud monk thinks of himself as
singular and exceptional. He is inclined to fast more, pray
longer, sleep less, look sicker than his fellows, proving that he is a
singularly holy man. Whatever must be done in common with his
brothers automatically loses its luster. "He is more pleased with
himself for having fasted once when the rest of the community
were eating a normal meal, than he is for having fasted a whole
week with the rest of the monastery. He finds more value in one
little private devotion, than in the whole of Matins and Lauds
sung in choir."* Such a monk feels his own speciality like an
ointment on the skin.

In the New Testament, the Pharisees as a party symbolized this
specific form of pride. Repelled by the profanity of the world, the
Pharisee sought sanctuary from the vulgarities of the common
life. He retreated into the inner community of law and virtue.
But it would be a singularly pharisaical reading of the story of
the Pharisees if one sought to show how modern democrats are
exempted from the sin of secession. Each in his own way may be
tempted to seek privileged sanctuary from a profane world. The
intellectual retreats from the mediocrities of mass culture into
the inner community of taste. The liberal retreats from the
moral failures of those who are wielders of power into the inner
community of criticism and virtue. The reactionary retreats into
impossible dreams about a bygone past to escape physical contact
with, and responsibility for, the present. The academic retreats
from the simplicities of the common life into the complexities of
his expertise.

* St. Bernard, *The Steps of Humility*, trans. Geoffrey Webb and Adrian
Walker (London: H. R. Mowbray and Co. Ltd., 1957), p. 69.

Less obvious but more significant than any of these forms of withdrawal, however, is the institution of modern marriage. One of the special features of a successful modern marriage is that it offers the comforts and pleasures of a "pharisaical" community. We have in mind here something more basic than the smug and self-congratulatory tone that can mar the successful marriage. This is the way in which a man can look upon his marriage as offering nothing more than a haven against the pressures of the profane world outside. The wife (or mistress) offers him retreat and sanctuary from a harsh environment. She provides a little comfort station where band-aids can be applied to one another's wounds, damaged pride restored, and the door shut now and then against the howling winds outside.

Where is the sin in such domestic comforts—all of them understandable and pitiable enough? Where is the pride? Not all the forms of pride are heroic. Not all pride consists in overt claims to divine power. Beneath the most unheroic expressions of self-pity can lurk no less stubborn a claim to one's own divinity. The high estimate of the self in this case is based on a pretension to divine virtue rather than divine power. The man who drenches himself with self-pity is convinced that underneath it all he is a splendid fellow, a rather precious innocent, much abused or neglected by a harsh environment in which he is trapped. No longer believing that he can conquer the world, he now simply seeks peace, release, and sanctuary from its blows.

Pride generates not only sins against the neighbor but also various sins of deception. In St. Augustine's words, pride is both cold and blind. The coldness of pride has already been observed. It shows up in condescending philanthropy just as surely as in the strategies of conquest and withdrawal. But pride means blindness as well as coldness. It means deception in one's dealings with God, the neighbor, and the self.

We have already spoken of deception concerning God. The prideful man misinterprets the nature of God. In aiming to replace God, he misplaces God; he seeks him where he is not. But no less certainly the prideful man is involved in deception with respect to his neighbor. In this regard, there is a double blindness in pride. First, the proud man has a distorted view of his neighbor. He no longer sees him as a companion before God. Wholly absorbed in his own effort at security, comfort, and salvation, he lets his neighbor fall into the background of his life while his own religious drama occupies the foreground. The neighbor may have an important place in this drama, but he appears only in the role assigned to him, after the major role has been cast. The major role in the drama, by definition, is the one that the man of pride has chosen to play. It alone is invested with an ultimate significance and all the rest serves as background, audience, and cue. In pride there is some of the blindness to others of the egocentric actor for whom nothing really matters except his own part and performance in the play.

The proud man also tries to give the neighbor a distorted view of himself. Under the pressure of pride, and under the even greater pressure of the futility of pride, he seeks to deceive his neighbor. St. Paul called it boasting or self-glorying. The man of pride seeks to support his own claims for himself in and through the neighbor. He boasts, he rationalizes, he justifies, in order to give size and symmetry to a self-expansion which not even he himself can wholly credit. Having turned away from the light and become his own light, he seeks out mirrors that will reflect and mutiply his somewhat uncertain brilliance. As it was already suggested in the chapter on deceit, this phenomenon is not so much a particular lie or exaggeration designed to mislead or impress as boasting and rationalization as a way of life in which there is a general expansion of one's borders.

Reinhold Niebuhr has rightly observed, however, that self-deception is even more fundamental to pride than the deception of the neighbor. "While . . . deception is constantly directed against competing wills, seeking to secure their acceptance and validation of the self's too generous opinion of itself, its primary purpose is to deceive, not others, but the self."[*] With this observation, Niebuhr continues the tradition from Augustine, Bernard, Thomas, and forward, in which it is recognized that the man of pride primarily deceives, and seeks to deceive, himself. "How easy it will be," declares Bernard, "for self-love to deceive

[*] Reinhold Niebuhr, *The Nature and Destiny of Man* (2 Pts.; London: Nisbet, 1941), Pt. I, chap. vii, p. 216.

you in your judgment of yourself." Niebuhr simply adds the shrewd observation that the need to deceive his neighbor only reveals that a man is not wholly successful in securing his own self-deception. In short, self-love is both blind and yet striving to be blind. The sin that begins in rebellion against God ends up in spiritual contention against the self.

Pride is self-deceiving for the further reason that it feeds on the validity of self-identity, rejecting obsequiousness and tentativeness. It does not seek to hide behind the irresponsibility of the passive voice. The church cannot oppose the untruth of pride with anything less than the whole truth; no weak definition of love and humility, in which the strength of self-identity is deleted, will suffice.

The blindness of pride is reinforced by its special invisibility as a sin. This peculiarity of pride stands out in comparison with other of the seven deadly sins. Malice, envy, lust, and avarice are visible in the evil works they produce. But pride can inspire good works as well as evil works. Indeed, it is especially the sin of good works. To put it in Luther's language: men are continually tempted by two devils—the black devil and the white devil. The strategy of the black devil is obvious. He tempts men to break the law. But the white devil is subtler, somewhat more difficult to see. He tempts men to obey the law, and then to glory in their obedience; to seize power and then to invest their seizure with a redemptive significance for others. Pride is the sin of the virtuous and the successful, the righteous and the law-abiding. It is hard to detect, not only because of its collaboration with virtue, but also because, although recognizable in others, it is peculiarly self-blinding. There is a sense, of course, in which all sin is blinding. For example, we speak of a person blind with lust or with rage. But pride is not only self-justification, but the self-justification which we do not see; it is always located behind one's back. When the devil tempts to lust, perhaps he appears in alluring costume, but when he tempts to pride, he always appears as one's own bland self.

There is, of course, an important historical argument against the invisibility of pride. It has been offered in varying forms by such diverse persons as St. Augustine, Reinhold Niebuhr,

Jacques Maritain, and Albert Camus. These men would readily admit that pride is pre-eminently the sin of the righteous and law-abiding. But they have gone on to observe a certain dialectical pattern in behavior and history, according to which the sins of the white devil inevitably produce the most serious sins of the black. The law-abiding eventually become the lawbreakers; the self-righteous become the unrighteous; the self-justifiers eventually justify murder. The vast majority of killings in the twentieth century have been committed not by lawbreakers who lived explicitly beyond the pale of the law, but, terrifyingly enough, by those who were officers of the law performing their duties to the state. In this sense, then, the invisible becomes visible as pride leads to murder.

Clearly we have not denied (and cannot) the fact of progression from pride to murder. Indeed, it has been one of the special concerns of this essay to explore the relation of pride to aggression in the human sphere. At the same time, it would be wrong to exploit this progression, as some have done, by building it up into a kind of argument for the Christian doctrine of the sinfulness of man. That the Christian must confess the pride in his aggression does not mean that aggression is the only mode of his pride. Pride has not always led to murder. It has not always been a threat to civilization. Indeed, proud men, in the theological sense of the term, have often managed to be philanthropists and music lovers, bridgebuilders and wildlife preservers. Not all the works of pride display themselves with an immediate harmfulness in the human sphere. This historical inconspicuousness also belongs to the invisibility of pride. In pride, the self, with all its loves and fears, its philanthropies and its conspiracies, terminates in itself. Its terminal connections with God are dead. But that this is the case is not always unambiguously clear.

The redemption of the righteous

There is good reason to ask whether the Word of God offers any hope whatsoever to the prideful. It might be argued that salvation does not come their way at all. The Savior seeks out those who live beyond the pale of the law—the adulterers, the thieves, the tax collectors, the ritually unclean. How often does he seek out the self-righteous themselves? He singles out in parable the lost sheep, the lost coin, the Samaritan, the prodigal son. Is there not an undeniable pathos in the teachings of the Savior toward the lost and the defeated? While forgiving the unrighteous, does he not pass over the self-righteous? "I came not to call the righteous, but sinners," he says. This announcement, it would seem, has its fulfillment on the Cross when he dies the death of the unrighteous, under the eyes of a righteous Jerusalem and Rome. To what degree, then, can it really be said that Golgotha is addressed to the prideful and the successful? Is it not a restricted affair between Christ and the defeated of the world, enclosing them in the love of God, while excluding the exclusive, snubbing the snobs, judging the judges, and banishing them, once and for all, from the reach of his love? Where, in short, has Christ appeared not only as judge but also as forgiver and helper and comforter of this sinner, the chief of sinners, the man, whose sin is the fount and destination of all sins, the man of pride?

There is, as a matter of fact, a most striking account of Christ's appearance to such a man. He was by his own admission a Pharisee, "educated according to the strict manner of the law," so fastidious and so zealous for the law of God, in fact, that he persecuted the Christians. Specifically, he sent them to prison and, on one occasion, watched with approval while one of them was stoned to death. This was a man whom Christ counted among his persecutors. His name, of course, was Saul.

It is the appearance of Christ to Saul that explicitly forbids the restriction of the Christian hope to the lawless and persecuted. With his appearance to Saul, he approaches also the law-abiding and the persecutors. There can be no further doubt that he dies for sinners, for he dies even for the chief of sinners, the man of pride. Moreover, he addresses the prideful with the full weight of his message. He comes to Saul with judgment: "Saul, Saul, why do you persecute me?" (Acts 22:7); but he promises him also his forgiveness: "Rise and be baptized, and wash away your sins. . . ."

(Acts 22:16) He comes to Saul with a commission, "Rise, and go into Damascus, and there you will be told all that is appointed for you to do" (Acts 22:10). And he bestows upon him the gifts of sight and power. " 'Brother Saul, the Lord Jesus who appeared to you on the road by which you came, has sent me that you may regain your sight and be filled with the Holy Spirit.' And immediately something like scales fell from his eyes and he regained his sight. Then he rose and was baptized, and took food and was strengthened" (Acts 9:17–19). The appearance of the risen Christ to Saul makes it clear that the Crucifixion is not simply an expression of a tragic bond of sympathy between God and the defeated of the world. The Savior comes on a mission of conquest in which sin is judged and killed, even in its most virulent and unsympathetic form. He has died for all sinners—not only for the unrighteous but also for the self-righteous—to embrace and reclothe them both in the love of God.

Here, ultimately, is the most important reason why the chapter on pride has been reserved to the end. Its location has less to do, finally, with its rank as a sin than with the question of the full scope and reach of divine grace.

Normally when Christians are concerned to bear witness to the length and breadth of God's grace, they try to show that Christ came not only to the law-abiding, but also to the lawbreakers, not only to the righteous but to the unrighteous, not only to the respectable but to the disreputable. It seems to me, however, that the problem of witnessing to the full compass of grace is quite the reverse. It is a question of showing that he came not only to the lawbreakers but to the law-abiding, not only to the unrighteous but to the self-righteous, not only to the disreputable but to the respectable, not only to the prostitute but to Saul. Only in this way is it clear that redemption has come the full distance to man, to the very destination of sin itself, where stands the man of pride, the tiresome lordly "I." "I did this because . . ." "I can't stand her . . ." "I'm unbelievably tired tonight . . ." "God I'd love to get my hands on that . . ." "I don't give a damn . . ." Even this "I," in its extremity and solitude, is addressed by the word of salvation.

12 The Shadow of Death:
SLOTH

I have paired sloth and pride because each in its own way points to sin's destination: pride to solitude and sloth to death. Sloth can be defined in two ways: according to its common-sense meaning, it is laziness; according to its theological definition, boredom. In what sense, then, is it the destination of sin? Is it the sleep of the lazy or the death of the bored?

At the level of common-sense definition, the slothful man is one who avoids work. He likes his holidays. On six days God labored, but on the seventh he rested. The lowly aim of the slothful man is to extend the Sabbath rest. If he works, he works to avoid work. His basic commitment in life is to peace, relaxation, and inactivity; since death is a state of total inactivity, sloth is the sin most like death. It brings sluggishness to its near perfection; as the store is closed, the shades are drawn, work stands still, and the keeper lies down to rest without will or way to rise again.

Sloth, even in this sense of laziness, was a rather important sin in the early church, particularly in the monasteries. The religious vocation meant a withdrawal from the workaday world. Although this withdrawal was for the sake of the more intense work of contemplation, it often meant a slump into total inactivity for the monk in the loneliness of his cell. In his writings on monastic practices, Cassian observes that sloth assails a man most acutely at certain hours of the day. Who can doubt it? He has only to mention the fact and one can imagine pious heads nodding in monasteries all over Europe and the Near East. The great brown bear drowses in all of us, the spirit of hibernation, so profound, so soothing.

In medieval society, however, work did not possess the redemptive significance it later enjoyed. Work was important for the maintenance of life, and it had aesthetic and liturgical value as a means to the adornment and celebration of life, but it was never seriously esteemed as a source of world transformation.

Not until the Industrial Revolution and afterward was it possible to look upon work as a redemptive instrument through which the world might be reconstructed. For the first time in Western history a considerable body of men could think not simply of providing for the necessities of life but of opening up new possibilities, not simply of getting on in the world, but of getting ahead; and—even more important—for the first time such hopes could be extended to whole societies. As worker, man was no longer a maintenance man; he was the source of world transformation. *Homo religiosus* and *homo sapiens* were replaced in public esteem by *homo faber*. Understandably enough, all those who shared confidence in the redemptive power of work tended to rank idleness high among the sins.

Consequently, among the more dedicated of Victorian capitalists, sloth was not simply one sin among others but the most dangerous of sins. For any civilization dedicated to work—driven by the doctrine of justification by work—idleness is an obscenity. It leads men out of the safe, secure, predictable workshop into the lurid temptations outside. For the Victorian, sloth was not so much the dead end of inactivity as the doorway to illegitimate activities. On the other side of that doorway a man was subject to frivolity, license, lust, and criminality; not surprisingly, some Victorian moralists viewed all play—including the play of children—with alarm.

In the twentieth century, of course, homilies against sloth in

---

* Admittedly there was some preparation for this high estimate of work in the Reformed tradition. Calvin's God, first and foremost, was a worker, as he governed the world in every detail; and Calvin's ethic was an ethic of work. But Calvin did not glorify work as the instrument of redemption. Admittedly, in certain respects, human work was a means to the transformation of the world, but not in the sense that it might surpass a work of redemption already accomplished. Not work, but God's work, was to be glorified by work. Man, not work, was to be served by work.

the capitalistic West have diminished in number. Society has moved beyond the compulsions of a work culture to the problems of a leisure culture—and not without some evidence that the fears of the Victorians were partly justified. At the same time, the Marxist East has fallen heir to the earlier traditions of the bourgeois West on the subject of work and sloth. Work once again has been invested with a religious significance and sloth held up as one of the chief sins. The meanings of work and sloth, of course, have been reinterpreted. Work is no longer proof of individual "calling" and "character"; rather it is the source of all social value, the revolutionary appropriation of which makes way for the redeemed community. Moreover, the concept of significant work has been broadened to include not simply the daily labors of men but also political action—that whole range of revolutionary action necessary to allow a society to enter into its full inheritance. Correspondingly, the concept of sloth has been broadened to include not only sloth at the workbench but also political apathy—that slumbering political consciousness of the proletariat which is one of the chief obstacles to revolutionary advance.*

Whether in its nineteenth-century capitalist or twentieth-century Communist versions, sloth is prominent among the vices. Work is shouldering the adversities coefficient to the pursuit of all serious ends. These may lie in the projection of a solitary, successful, brilliant career, as in the case of the capitalist, or in the establishment of a thriving collective, as in the case of the Communist; but in either case, the slothful man sins because he refuses to assume these burdens.

No doubt there are insights of value to Christian reflection in these recent developments on the subject of sloth. First, the high evaluation of work made by both capitalist and Communist is

---

* Once the revolution has taken place, of course, there is little to distinguish the Communist homily on sloth from its earlier Victorian counterpart. For the Communist leader, political apathy can be a convenience rather than an obstacle, insofar as it minimizes the threat of counterrevolutionary activity. Sloth therefore returns to its narrower definition as a slump in productivity at the workbench.

not without its tie to the Christian ideal of service to the neighbor. A responsible, accountable life before God includes a sense
of responsibility to the brother. The Christian God, after all, is
one who united himself to human flesh. To attend to this God is
to attend to the brother and his needs. Second, social reformers
have helped to remind the Christian moralist that laziness has
many forms, not all of which can be reduced to irresponsibility at
the workbench. Apathy in politics, just as surely as in business,
may be an expression of neglect toward the neighbor and his
good.

However, it is not yet clear that the theological notion of sloth
can be reduced to recent Western homilies against laziness. There
is, after all, a striking cultural alternative to the Western ideal,
according to which inactivity is less sin than salve, less hurtful
than healing. The sophisticated religious traditions of the East
have made sloth—in the sense of detachment from activity—
man's only sure escape from the frenzied pursuit of idols. Recently, even members of the middle class in the West, that social
class which has been most committed to the doctrine of justification by work, has shown signs of disenchantment with the ideal
of relentless activity. As though with a view to their self-preserva-
tion and sanity, men seek out those ceremonies—the warm bath,
the cocktail before dinner, the outdoor cookout, an evening of
television—that will mercifully interrupt the frenzied pace of life
and help them momentarily recover some of the oblivion and self-
composure of the garden slug. The widespread appeal of these
cultural alternatives suggests that the West has been somewhat
too messianic in its claims for work, and therefore a little too
hysterical in its judgments against laziness.

Sloth as dejection, boredom, or apathy

According to classical theological definition, sloth is not simply
laziness, although St. Thomas, for example, observes that it "implies a certain weariness of work."* According to the Fathers of

* *ST* II. ii. q 35 art. 1.

the Church, who first listed it among the seven capital sins, sloth is not laziness so much as *acedia*—dejection or melancholy. John of Damascus defines the sin as an oppressive grief, but it is not what we would call today a general medical state of depression, which is indeterminate as to object; Thomas Aquinas specifies the peculiar object of this grief when he calls it "sorrow in the Divine Good." *

But what is the cause of this grief over the divine good that concerns the medieval moralist? There are two possibilities. First, and less seriously, a man may grieve over the loss or absence of a good that he desires. Thus, a father may lament the loss of his son; a lover, the death of his beloved; or a religious man, the absence of God. This form of dejection is not hopeless because there is the possibility of its annulment—if and when the man who is grieved is restored to his good. Far more serious, however, is the condition of the man who is melancholic and dejected in the very presence of the good. Such a man has his son, but his son bores him. He possesses his beloved, but he finds her incapable of stirring his interest. He has been promised the presence of God, but this promise leaves him cold. To such a man the presence or absence of the good makes no difference. His desire for the good is dead. Sometimes, of course, in the first throes of his dejection, he may think his grief is caused by the loss of the good, and pine and sigh for its return. But the most depressing recognition is that such a return would change nothing; his fundamental difficulty is an interior deadness of soul.

Apathy would be a better term to describe this profound dejection. The soul in this state is beyond mere sadness and melancholy. It has removed itself from the rise and fall of feelings; the very root of its feelings in desire is dead. That is why, for the medieval moralist, sloth was, in a sense, the most terrifying of sins. It is sin at its uttermost limit. To be a man is to desire. The good man desires God and other things in God. The sinful man desires things in the place of God, but he is still recognizably human, inasmuch as he knows desire. The slothful man, how-

* *Ibid.*, art. 2.

ever, is a dead man, an arid waste. He is medieval man in his extremity; his desire itself has dried up.

This spiritual condition, to which the medieval church was particularly sensitive, has also commanded the attention of later Christian moralists. It is somewhat like the predicament of a starving man. He needs food desperately, but cannot keep it on his stomach. Similarly, a man in the worst of spiritual straits remains unmoved even before the good of God; this is what St. John of the Cross referred to as the dark night of the soul. In his extremity a man experiences not simply the absence of God but a terrifying dryness and darkness which, it seems to him, not even the presence of God could assuage; his desire for God goes dead.

Kierkegaard, in the *Concept of Dread,* described that de-moniac state in which the soul, shivering in uninterest before the intrusion of the good, cries with the demon, "What have I to do with thee, O Jesus of Nazareth, holy one of God?" Later, James Joyce remembered enough of his Roman Catholicism to picture that same state of removal and withdrawal in the figure of Stephen Dedalus:

> By his monstrous way of life he seemed to have put himself beyond the limits of reality. Nothing moved him or spoke to him from the real world. . . . He could respond to no earthly or human appeal, dumb and insensible to the call of summer and gladness and companionship, wearied and dejected by his father's voice.*

Such is the experience of sloth at its profoundest level—a spiritual deadness or numbness so complete that one's "soul ceases to be refreshed by the fountains of sanctifying grace."**

Perhaps boredom is the best modern term to characterize this deadness of soul. But this state must not be confused with what the modern sophisticate means when he says he is bored. The latter obviously feels that his environment has let him down.

---

* James Joyce, *A Portrait of the Artist as a Young Man* (New York: Signet Books, 1949), p. 70.
** *Ibid.*

Once he may have turned to a lovely girl, to a sunlit holiday, or to a new possession with a certain zest and hopefulness. But the woman turns out to be less interesting in fact than in fantasy; the long-awaited holiday is not the lyrical interlude he expects it to be; and the eagerly awaited possession loses its luster once it is installed in the home. All objects successively fail him. If he feels a sense of personal responsibility for incurring these disappointments, it is not that he has failed these objects but rather that he has betrayed himself by allowing himself to become foolishly enthusiastic. His subsequent boredom, then, is the sober recovery of himself. Unresponsiveness is the only fitting attitude in a world that has lost its splendor.

In the sin of sloth, however, the situation is quite the reverse. In boredom before God, it is man who has failed his object, and not the reverse. Although the modern sophisticate feels no need to apologize for being bored—his attitude, after all, merely reflects the poverty of his object—the man of faith must confess his boredom as his sin because his attitude reflects the poverty of his own soul. To be unmoved and untouched in the presence of God exposes an interior inadequacy.

Sloth in liturgy and theology

The liturgical expression of the sin of sloth is the Protestant worship service. The very posture of the worshipers suggests boredom as they settle themselves lethargically in their seats. Each item in the service—hymns, prayers, and sermon—is self-contained, static, and ponderous, installed, as it were, in its own pew. There is no joyous movement in the course of the service from episode to episode or from place to place. It becomes an effort for the worshiper, once or twice in the length of an hour, to hoist his dead weight to a standing position for song. No handclapping, no disputes, no interruptions, no dancing, no shouting, no joy. A man does not need to be a Pentecostal sectarian to find the atmosphere boring. Revealingly enough, historic Trinitarian faith insisted that prayers should be offered standing rather than kneeling (Council of Nicea, Canon 20). With this directive, the Church Fathers recognized the liturgical implications of their own Trinitarian affirmations. The church celebrates a God alive —Father, Son, and Holy Spirit.

The theological basis for this slothful atmosphere in worship is a defective sense of the glory of God. The act of worship, after all, is the act of "glorifying" God; it is the human reflex before the divine glory. But it is precisely a sense of his glory that is lacking in much contemporary Protestant theology. While Protestants maintain a sense of God as their transcendent Lord, they have not often reflected in their theology and preaching a powerful sense of his glory. The consequence is sloth.

The term glory has specific associations with the experience of both life and light. Even at the level of ordinary contact with objects, boredom indicates a failure to encounter glory. A man finds a subject boring because for him it is both deadly and dull. Conversely, something is glorious if it is both lustrous and richly alive. The Hebrew word for the glory of God (*kabod*) refers to the light of his appearance, to his splendor, his weight, his wealth, and the concrete fullness of his life.** In the New Testament both light and life are ascribed to Jesus Christ and to the Holy Spirit; in Christ men behold the glory of God, and by the Spirit men are capable of this beholding. If Christ, then, is the light and life of God incarnate, the Holy Spirit is the illuminator and life-giver, by virtue of which men participate in God's glory. When, therefore, Christian preaching and theology are dull, they are quite literally spiritless. They are vague, abstract, empty— and justifiably boring—whenever they fail to convey a sense of the actual appearance, or shining forth, of God and of the full wealth of his life, in which he makes himself known.

Karl Barth has attempted to remind us of this fullness of divine life and light by appealing to another biblical phrase: the

* See Arthur C. McGill, *Celebration of Flesh: Poetry in Christian Life* (New York: Association Press, 1964), pp. 182–184, for a lighthearted account of the ponderous, boring liturgies of the Protestant churches.

** See especially Edmond Jacob, *Theology of the Old Testament*, trans. Arthur W. Heathcote and Philip J. Allcock (London: Hodder and Stoughton, 1958), pp. 79–82.

"Lord of hosts." If the term "Lord" refers to the sovereign transcendence of God, then the plural term "hosts" insures that this
transcendence will not be misconceived as remote and empty.
There is a plenitude in the divine being, which the plural alone
conveys.* Monotheism runs thin whenever it ignores the wealth
and abundance of the divine life. It is not enough for theologians
to assert the bare existence of God. Theology that is alive to its
object, and preaching that is not bored and boring, must enter
into the plurality of the divine name. They must reckon with the
kabod of God, with the variety of his perfections and with the
multitude of his works:

> Sing to the Lord, bless his name;
> tell of his salvation from day to day.
> Declare his glory among the nations,
> his marvelous works among all the peoples!
> For great is the Lord, and greatly to be praised. . . .
>
> Psalm 96:2–4

Preachers and theologians who fall short of this testimony to the
glory of God are guilty of the sin of sloth; their work is rife with
unbelief.

A certain one-sided development in twentieth-century neo-
orthodox Protestant theology makes the point clear. Modern neo-
orthodoxy has reacted against an earlier liberalism by insisting
upon the radical distinction between God and the world. It has
reasserted, in effect, the supremacy of the Lord over every human
glory. This reaffirmation, of course, was an attempt to correct a
nineteenth-century idealist tradition that had reduced God to
the achievements of man and the splendors of this world. However needful this reaction may have been, it contained its own
danger. The transcendent God, if abstracted from his own inner
glory, becomes a cipher, a spectral figure, a mere negative limit to
thought and action, devoid of any positive content of his own.
Unable to attend to this abstraction, and secretly bored with this
God, theological reflection must eventually turn away from God

---

* Both Barth and Jacob argue that the glory of God refers not to a single
perfection or attribute of God but to the full array of his perfections. Karl
Barth, *Church Dogmatics*, ed. G. W. Bromiley and T. F. Torrance (12 Vols.;
Edinburgh: T. & T. Clark, 1956), II, 324 ff.

and concentrate upon man, but this time not in his glory but in his shame, defeat, and sin. This is what happened in neo-orthodox thought. The doctrine of the sinfulness of man became the major assertion in theology, upon which all other assertions, including the affirmation of God's existence, depended. Consequently, any weakening of the sense of man's sinfulness might render God dispensable. No sin, no God; this is the odd logic of those whose affirmation of God's existence depends entirely upon their sense of sin. The resurgence—or the apparent resurgence—of a "new optimism" about man in the 1960's has led some ex-neo-orthodox theologians to proclaim once again that God is dead. For such bored theologians, God's existence was not linked with his own showing forth of himself as the lord of hosts, the king of glory.

There is no reason, however, to speak about this development as though boredom is a sin from which all others are exempted. Like all other sins, its logic is both plausible and highly tempting; after all, the glory of God does not unveil itself to man directly and immediately. The naked eye sees only a child born in a stable, and a man dying on a cross. Where indeed is the lord of glory? Only by faith can a man say that the light, the abundance, and the life of God has shown itself in the face of Jesus Christ, and that this glory is sufficient to render boredom inexcusable, to make delight possible, and to open the way to a modest pleasure in the several earthly glories that man knows. It might appear far more reasonable to seek one's glory elsewhere—perhaps in the explosion of galaxies, in the flash of human creativity, or in the changing colors of the political scene. And if, in their turn, these secondary glories fail, it may seem altogether appropriate to sink into a state of total apathy in which the soul is divested of all enthusiasms whatsoever.

Progression in sloth toward the destination of sin

Two stages may be distinguished in the development of sloth; boredom with God, and boredom with the world. In its first stage, boredom is a generic feature of all sin; in its second stage, it is the special terminal sin of sloth. When man turns away from God to some other god, he gives evidence of his boredom with God by seeking light, abundance, and life elsewhere. In this sense, sloth is a generic feature of all sin. But sin has not yet reached its destination. Only when—his desires played out, his taste grown stale—a man has exhausted the glory of creaturely powers is boredom his in the special, terminal sense of the term. The destination of sin reveals itself in a final state of atrophy.

This progression in sloth parallels the development in pride. For this reason, also, the two sins have been paired in this series of essays under the rubric of "the destination of sin." Each in its own way is an element in sin at its beginning and once again, more especially, at its end. Pride represents man's denial of God's lordship. In the first stages of pride a man rebels against the Lord, but he may do so by handing himself over to other lordly powers. In the later stages, a man completes this process of rebellion as he subordinates all other powers to the lordship of the solitary self. But sin is not only a revolt against the Lord; it is also a defection from his glory. In the first stages of this defection, a man turns toward other powers that attract through their glory; but, in its terminal stages, a man finds himself incapable of exuberance toward any powers whatsoever. In effect, the idol has fallen away, not only with respect to its lordship but also with respect to its glory. The solitary self to which pride is devoted in its final stages is at one and the same time the bored self. It was Kierkegaard who observed that "the demoniacal is the vacuous, the tedious."* The devil, above all else, is bored.

As St. Paul put it, the wages of sin is death: boredom is simply and pre-eminently that sin in which payment is not deferred. Ultimately, of course, the foretaste of death must be acknowledged in all other sins if sloth as spiritual death is in fact their destination. Boredom will simply disclose the spiritual immanence of death in them all. Dorothy Sayers once divided the various capital sins into the cold and the warm. She included pride, avarice, envy, and sloth among the cold sins and gluttony, lust, and anger among the warm. It is not too farfetched to

---

* Søren Kierkegaard, *The Concept of Dread*, trans. Walter Lowrie (Princeton: Princeton University Press, 1946), p. 118.

recognize in Miss Sayers' typology the two classic images for
death—a fiery destruction and a cold corpse. In the course of
these essays we have inevitably used both images for expressing
man's relation to the sins. In idolatry, lust, and anger, one thinks
of a man as possessed, consumed, burned up, or burned out by
the powers to which he is enthralled. In pride, envy, avarice,
betrayal, faintheartedness, and neglect, one thinks of a man as
numb, cold, and withdrawn. The second line of images is more
terrifying, of course, because it stands in a terminal relationship
to the first. When the last fire burns out, a sin terminates in a
coldness of soul that is death. For this reason sloth points to the
destination of sin better than any of the others. It signifies that
spiritual condition wherein every vital impulse toward God and
the neighbor is dead. Among the sins, sloth is the last sign on the
road to death.

Easter and Pentecost

The bestowal of his life upon men would fail to reach its goal
if Christ had not placed himself first in full solidarity with men
in the extremity of their death. In its extremity, we have seen,
sloth is not simply the mild foretaste of dying that men experience
in sleep, nor the sharper confrontation with death that they know
in bereavement. Rather it is that death which has overtaken the
soul before its death, when the soul itself is dead, when it
responds with equal disinterest to the presence of friend or foe,
God or devil alike. This is sloth in its worst form, not as it attacks
at certain times of the day (Matthew 26:30–46) nor as it assails in
mourning (John 20:19–31) but as it extends inward and outward,
backward and forward, touching everything with gloom like a
November rain.

In a sense, such spiritual death is no human experience at all.
As Kierkegaard well understood, it represents the outer limit of
sin, its demonic extremity (Mark 5:7). Yet it ought not to be
supposed that it occurs in a domain that God has not already
made his own. While there is no event to suggest explicitly that

Jesus experienced the sort of apathy that we have described, Scripture does report that the Son of man lay in a grave, as dead as any man, before or after him, cold to the bone, and that three days before this he grieved in Gethsemane, not an ordinary passing grief, but the grief that does not pass, the grief which is "even unto death." It ought not to be supposed therefore that God is far off, remote and helpless, while men alone have touched death, shuddered before it outwardly and within. Far from it, it may be that men have known death only from the outside as it were—like sleepy disciples in Gethsemane, like centurions posted outside the grave of Joseph of Arimathea—while the son of God has confronted death directly from within. And he has done so, not in order to sink ineffectively into death or into its spiritual antecedent, apathy, adding perhaps a little note of religious sympathy to the overriding gloom, but rather to break open the graves of the self-entombed and to bring them alive to their feet in the presence of God.

The irruption of the Holy Spirit in the community has the power to enliven men and illumine them when they are most tempted to apathy in the course of the journey. Jesus himself bestowed the Spirit on the church; and it is revealing that he did so precisely at that moment when the Disciples were tempted to sink into depression over his disappearance from their midst.

Significantly, the Holy Spirit is characterized in the New Testament as the Comforter (or Advocate), the Life-Giver, and the Spirit of Truth. These various names for the Spirit, rightly understood, summarize everything that has been said on the subject of sloth. First, the Spirit is comforter (John 14:15, 26; 15:26; 16:7). As comforter and advocate, the Spirit attacks sloth in its less severe form of dejection over the loss of the good. Jesus promises the Spirit as the continuing, counseling presence of God in the crisis of his own imminent absence.* The Son of God has not simply made a cosmic getaway in his own death and resurrection. His future presence may be indirect rather than direct, by faith rather than by sight, but it will be no less real. The Spirit

* John 16:6.

will remain with men just as a comforter might offer compassion to his friend in grief, a counselor make his presence felt to a man in need, or an advocate stand by an accused.

The Spirit is also called the giver of life (II Corinthians 3:6). Dejection is not simply grief over the absence of the good; more profoundly it is apathy. The Spirit attacks the dejection of the church that is deadness of soul. The Apostle compares the life-giving power of the Spirit to a fruitful field whose harvest is "love, joy, peace, patience, kindness, goodness, faithfulness, gentleness, self-control."* This harvest is both a provision for life and a foretaste of the final harvest, eternal life (Galatians 6:8; Romans 8:11). Paul uses another image for life when he refers to "walking by the Spirit." The Holy Spirit inspirits; it would breathe life into sluggish Adam; it would raise him up, and teach his footsore, weary, laggard children how to run and to dance.

Finally, the Holy Spirit is also the spirit of truth. Men are not only raised to their feet to continue their journey, they are given a certain measure of illumination for the way. "If we live by the Spirit, let us also walk by the Spirit" (Galatians 5:25). The Spirit is life-giver only because it is the spirit of truth. Comfort is cruel if it is based on an illusion; counsel ruinous if it advances falsehood; life only collapses into death if it feeds off a lie. The Spirit is life-giver only because it leads men toward no dreamy illusion, no vaporous glory, but to the solid flesh of the Savior.

The limitations of a catalogue

Sloth belongs at the end of a catalogue of sins not only because it is the destination of sin but also because this placement helps to expose the limitations of any such catalogue. A cataloguer of sins runs the serious danger of impoverishing the Christian sense of grace.

First, by limiting himself to the subject of sin, he ignores, at least in part, the problem of suffering and death. To this degree,

---

* Galatians 5:22. See also Galatians 6:8.

he overlooks the grace of God as it reaches a suffering and dying, as well as a sinful, humanity. He fails to acknowledge the grace of God as it touches the whole of the human condition. He does not reckon with a salvation that enlivens dead men as well as rehabilitating sinful men.

Perhaps an incident from one of the novels of Dostoevski will serve to indicate the spiritual deficiency of a theology of grace which is restricted to the problem of sin. On one memorable occasion in *Crime and Punishment*, the hero, Raskolnikov, visits the prostitute, Sonya, in her squalid quarters. With mock deference, he kisses (and honors all suffering humanity in) her foot. Then with some cruelty, he prophesies one of three possible ends for her. One day, he predicts, she will either jump off a bridge, turn to stone, or go mad.

There is a striking consistency to the predictions. Raskolnikov does not moralize about a fall from virtue to vice; rather, he sees Sonya's destiny as a fall from life to death. She will either take her own life, become insensitive as stone, or suffer the destruction of her consciousness in madness. There is also a remarkable appropriateness to Sonya's reply. She does not leap to defend herself on moral grounds in the fashion of a Western girl—the storied prostitute with a heart of gold. She does not attempt to clothe herself with explanations: "I have done this because my father is a drunkard, my stepmother consumptive, and I have hungry brothers and sisters to feed." Instead, rejecting altogether the tediousness of moral defense, she reads to Raskolnikov from the eleventh chapter of the Gospel of John, the story of the raising of Lazarus from the dead.

The fall from life to death is her predicament; the Christ who raises the dead to life is her hope.

Dostoevski's insight is tacitly acknowledged by the placement of a chapter on sloth at the end of this series of essays. Man is sufferer as well as sinner, and the life of God addresses him in both aspects of his plight. Needless to say, the subject of sloth is not identical with the problem of death. It takes up only that deadness of soul which sin itself inwardly produces, but at least it

serves as a warning that there is more to the human condition
than sin itself.

Sloth is a sharp reminder that man's spiritual problem is not
simply a fall from righteousness to unrighteousness but from life
to death. Correspondingly, man's rehabilitation requires his
movement not only from unrighteousness to righteousness but
from death to life. Theologians impoverish the Christian sense of
salvation when they interpret it only moralistically, as the forgiveness and correction of sins. Salvation also means being raised
from the dead. No man knows this better than the man raised up
from apathy. God's love is not simply forgiving and corrective; it
is quickening and enlivening. This is the special instruction
about grace hidden in the depths of sloth.

There is a second way in which a catalogue of sins might
impoverish the sense of the grace of God were it not for the special
focus of an essay on sloth. Any book that begins with an analysis
of the human condition and then proceeds to a discussion of the
grace of God as it touches human needs gives the impression that
God's grace meets but does not exceed the problems to be solved.
God's power becomes perfectly proportional—or equal—to the
difficulties men face, but no more. Grace is trimmed to fit human
want; the rest is theological waste. The result is the triumphant
lord of neo-orthodox monotheism, who, for all his triumph, remains (beyond his coping with human problems) relatively abstract, bare, and impoverished: a cipher. This method, for all its
value, offers an altogether too parsimonious reckoning of the
divine glory; it leaves no room for the sheer exuberance of the
divine life that exceeds the economy of salvation. God's grace
infinitely surpasses the needs of man, both as sufferer and as
sinner. No man has experienced this surplus of grace more
vividly than the man raised up from apathy. Inasmuch as he has
been retrieved from boredom by a brilliant and life-giving object, he surely has discovered more in his object than the bare
fact that his boredom has been overcome. A study of sloth then
serves as a final reminder that there is more to celebrate in the
divine life than the conquest of sin and death.

Of the four ways in which men can talk about the surplus of divine grace, only one of them has been appropriate to this book. The first is the language of Apocalypse. The Revelation of St. John reckons with the glory of the Heavenly Jerusalem as it utterly exceeds the cramped cut of a man in his sin. " 'Behold, the dwelling of God is with men. He will dwell with them, and they shall be his people, and God himself will be with them; he will wipe away every tear from their eyes, and death shall be no more, neither shall there be mourning nor crying nor pain any more, for the former things have passed away' " (Revelation 21:3–4). The second is the language of worship. The prayers of the church include not only those shaped by human need—the prayers of confession, intercession, and thanksgiving—but also those that celebrate a glory that surpasses it—the prayers of adoration and praise. The third is the language of ethics. From one perspective, a phenomenology of the virtues might be interpreted as a discussion of the diverse ways in which men are invited to participate in the divine life. But this is the theme of a different sort of book.

In a volume restricted to the sins alone, there is only one way of suggesting that grace cannot be pared down to the patterns of sin; and this is through the language of comedy. The comedian and the apocalypticist are not far removed from one another in their sense of the eschatological reversal of all things. There is something ultimately ludicrous about human foible. However alluring, powerful, and plausible sin may appear, it is comically disproportionate to the power against which it contends. There is something unequal about the contest between God and the sinner, and only the mode of comedy does justice to their lack of equivalence and symmetry. While capturing a sense of the force of sin, comedy puts sin in its place, something which the perspective of systematic theology never achieves.

This is illustrated in the episode that occurs shortly before the passion of Jesus when he is assaulted by the mother of the sons of Zebedee, that breathtakingly ordinary and prosaic woman, who asks, "Command that these two sons of mine may sit, one at your right hand and one at your left, in your kingdom" (Matthew

20:21). Her request is sublimely out of place; the disciples, if anything, take her too seriously in the matter. They become indig-
nant. But Jesus answers:

> "You do not know what you are asking. Are you able to drink
> the cup that I am to drink?" They [the sons of Zebedee] said to
> him, "We are able." He said to them, "You will drink my cup,
> but to sit at my right hand and at my left is not mine to grant,
> but it is for those for whom it has been prepared by my
> Father."

And to the disciples he says:

> ". . . Whoever would be great among you must be your servant,
> and whoever would be first among you must be your slave;
> even as the Son of man came not to be served but to serve, and
> to give his life as a ransom for many."
>
> Matthew 20:22–23; 26–28

The kingdom of God is not pliant to the will of a woman am-
bitious for the advancement of her sons. The rule of God will
succeed and it will establish a kingdom in which the great shall be
servant and the first shall be slaves in the reversal of all things.
And yet Jesus does not establish a symmetrical contrast between
the two orders, indignantly defending God against the woman.
The comedy is completed and the orders put in their true perspective when this very woman reappears, ministering to Jesus at
the foot of the cross. This is the astonishment of grace.

About the Author

William F. May is professor and chairman of the new program in the study of religion at Indiana University. A graduate of Princeton University, he received his B.D. and Ph.D. degrees from Yale, and was chairman of the religion department at Smith College.

Dr. May is an ordained Presbyterian minister, a contributing editor of *Christianity and Crisis,* and a member of the Society for Religion in Higher Education. His essays on "Albert Camus: Political Moralist" and "Manichaeism in American Politics" were included in *Witness to a Generation,* a volume of significant writings taken from *Christianity and Crisis,* 1941–1966.